Table of Contents

Sections: Day:

(Answer Key in Back)

Name: _____

Score:

Rectangles and Squares

Perimeter

Add all the sides together.

$$Perimeter = L + L + W + W$$

Or

Length x2 + Width x2

$$Perimeter = L \times 2 + W \times 2$$

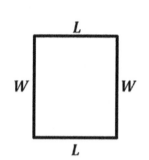

Area

Multiply the length by the width.

$$Area = L \times W$$

① Area = _____
Perimeter = _____

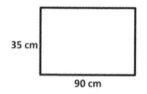

35 cm
90 cm

② Area = _____
Perimeter = _____

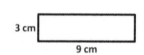

3 cm
9 cm

③ Area = _____
Perimeter = _____

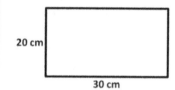

20 cm
30 cm

④ Area = _____
Perimeter = _____

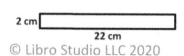

2 cm
22 cm

⑤ Area = _____
Perimeter = _____

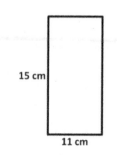

15 cm
11 cm

⑥ Area = _____
Perimeter = _____

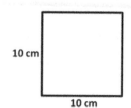

10 cm
10 cm

Day 2
Rectangles & Squares

Name: _____

Score:

① Area = _____
   Perimeter = _____

38 cm
16 cm

② Area = _____
   Perimeter = _____

9 cm
7 cm

③ Area = _____
   Perimeter = _____

2 cm
3 cm

④ Area = _____
   Perimeter = _____

7 cm
15 cm

⑤ Area = _____
   Perimeter = _____

15 cm
12 cm

⑥ Area = _____
   Perimeter = _____

14 cm
3 cm

⑦ Area = _____
   Perimeter = _____

17 cm
12 cm

⑧ Area = _____
   Perimeter = _____

33 cm
41 cm

⑨ Area = _____
   Perimeter = _____

6 cm
1 cm

Name: _____

Score:

① Area = _____
Perimeter = _____

22 cm | 22 cm

② Area = _____
Perimeter = _____

36 cm | 47 cm

③ Area = _____
Perimeter = _____

16 cm | 47 cm

④ Area = _____
Perimeter = _____

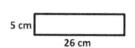
5 cm | 26 cm

⑤ Area = _____
Perimeter = _____

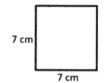
7 cm | 7 cm

⑥ Area = _____
Perimeter = _____

18 cm | 11 cm

⑦ Area = _____
Perimeter = _____

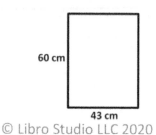
60 cm | 43 cm

⑧ Area = _____
Perimeter = _____

1 cm | 16 cm

⑨ Area = _____
Perimeter = _____

3 cm | 5 cm

Day 4
Rectangles & Squares

Name: _____

Score:

① Area = _____
Perimeter = _____

2 cm
2 cm

② Area = _____
Perimeter = _____

9 cm
3 cm

③ Area = _____
Perimeter = _____

6 cm
5 cm

④ Area = _____
Perimeter = _____

2 cm
5 cm

⑤ Area = _____
Perimeter = _____

8 cm
14 cm

⑥ Area = _____
Perimeter = _____

16 cm
16 cm

⑦ Area = _____
Perimeter = _____

5 cm
42 cm

⑧ Area = _____
Perimeter = _____

60 cm
45 cm

⑨ Area = _____
Perimeter = _____

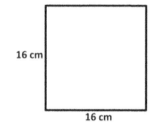

15 cm
10 cm

© Libro Studio LLC 2020

Name: _____

Score:

Triangles

Perimeter

Add all three sides together.
(side a + base + side c)

$Perimeter = a + b + c$

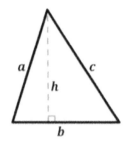

Area

One-half the base times the height.

$$Area = \frac{b \times h}{2}$$

---

① Area = _____

Perimeter = _____

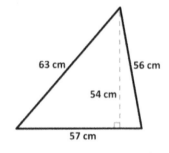

② Area = _____

Perimeter = _____

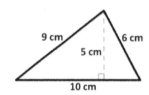

③ Area = _____

Perimeter = _____

---

④ Area = _____

Perimeter = _____

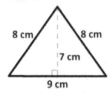

⑤ Area = _____

Perimeter = _____

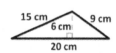

⑥ Area = _____

Perimeter = _____

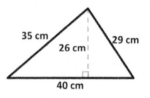

Day 6
Triangles

Name: _____

Score:

①
Area = _____
Perimeter = _____

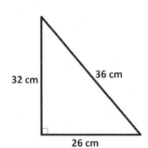

32 cm   36 cm   26 cm

②
Area = _____
Perimeter = _____

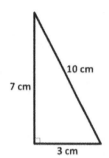

10 cm   7 cm   3 cm

③
Area = _____
Perimeter = _____

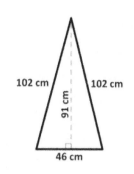

102 cm   102 cm   91 cm   46 cm

④
Area = _____
Perimeter = _____

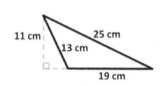

11 cm   25 cm   13 cm   19 cm

⑤
Area = _____
Perimeter = _____

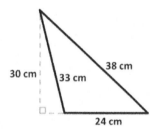

30 cm   33 cm   38 cm   24 cm

⑥
Area = _____
Perimeter = _____

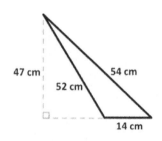

47 cm   54 cm   52 cm   14 cm

⑦
Area = _____
Perimeter = _____

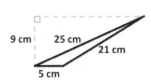

9 cm   25 cm   21 cm   5 cm

⑧
Area = _____
Perimeter = _____

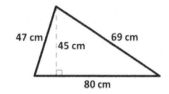

47 cm   69 cm   45 cm   80 cm

⑨
Area = _____
Perimeter = _____

9 cm   7 cm   11 cm   8 cm

Name: _____

Score:

① Area = _____
Perimeter = _____

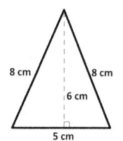

8 cm   8 cm
6 cm
5 cm

② Area = _____
Perimeter = _____

9 cm   8 cm   16 cm
14 cm

③ Area = _____
Perimeter = _____

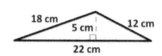

18 cm   5 cm   12 cm
22 cm

④ Area = _____
Perimeter = _____

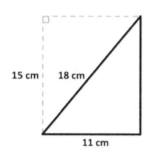

15 cm   18 cm
11 cm

⑤ Area = _____
Perimeter = _____

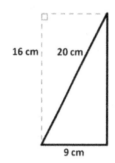

16 cm   20 cm
9 cm

⑥ Area = _____
Perimeter = _____

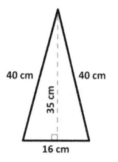

40 cm   35 cm   40 cm
16 cm

⑦ Area = _____
Perimeter = _____

7 cm   15 cm   9 cm
10 cm

⑧ Area = _____
Perimeter = _____

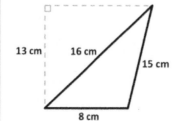

13 cm   16 cm   15 cm
8 cm

⑨ Area = _____
Perimeter = _____

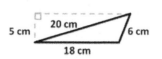

5 cm   20 cm   6 cm
18 cm

Name: _____

Score:

①
Area = _____
Perimeter = _____

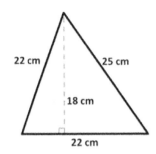
22 cm 25 cm 18 cm 22 cm

②
Area = _____
Perimeter = _____

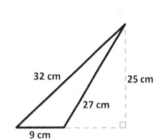
32 cm 25 cm 27 cm 9 cm

③
Area = _____
Perimeter = _____

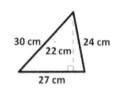
30 cm 24 cm 22 cm 27 cm

④
Area = _____
Perimeter = _____

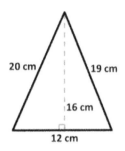
20 cm 19 cm 16 cm 12 cm

⑤
Area = _____
Perimeter = _____

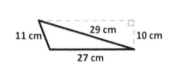
11 cm 29 cm 10 cm 27 cm

⑥
Area = _____
Perimeter = _____

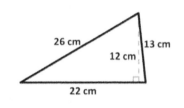
26 cm 13 cm 12 cm 22 cm

⑦
Area = _____
Perimeter = _____

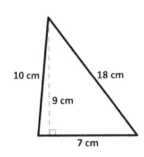
10 cm 18 cm 9 cm 7 cm

⑧
Area = _____
Perimeter = _____

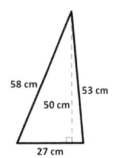
58 cm 53 cm 50 cm 27 cm

⑨
Area = _____
Perimeter = _____

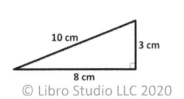
10 cm 3 cm 8 cm

Name: _____

Score:

① Area = _____
Perimeter = _____

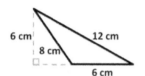
6 cm · 12 cm · 8 cm · 6 cm

② Area = _____
Perimeter = _____

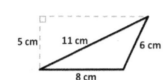
5 cm · 11 cm · 6 cm · 8 cm

③ Area = _____
Perimeter = _____

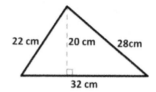
22 cm · 20 cm · 28cm · 32 cm

④ Area = _____
Perimeter = _____

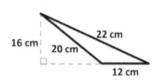
16 cm · 22 cm · 20 cm · 12 cm

⑤ Area = _____
Perimeter = _____

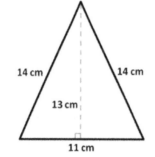
14 cm · 14 cm · 13 cm · 11 cm

⑥ Area = _____
Perimeter = _____

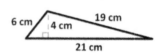
6 cm · 19 cm · 4 cm · 21 cm

⑦ Area = _____
Perimeter = _____

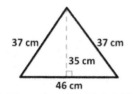
37 cm · 37 cm · 35 cm · 46 cm

⑧ Area = _____
Perimeter = _____

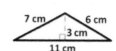
7 cm · 6 cm · 3 cm · 11 cm

⑨ Area = _____
Perimeter = _____

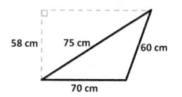
58 cm · 75 cm · 60 cm · 70 cm

Name: _____

Score:

Parallelograms

Perimeter

Add all the sides together.

Perimeter $= a + a + b + b$

Or

Perimeter $= a \times 2 + b \times 2$

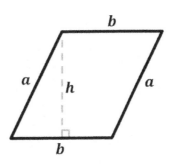

Area

Multiply the base by the height.

Area $= b \times h$

---

① Area = _____
  Perimeter = _____

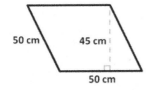

② Area = _____
  Perimeter = _____

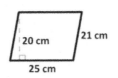

③ Area = _____
  Perimeter = _____

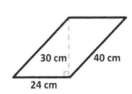

---

④ Area = _____
  Perimeter = _____

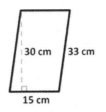

⑤ Area = _____
  Perimeter = _____

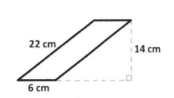

⑥ Area = _____
  Perimeter = _____

Day 11
Parallelograms

Name: _____

Score:

① Area = _____

Perimeter = _____

27 cm | 30 cm
44 cm

② Area = _____

Perimeter = _____

24 cm | 27 cm
52 cm

③ Area = _____

Perimeter = _____

11 cm / 9 cm
37 cm

④ Area = _____

Perimeter = _____

36 cm | 39 cm
27 cm

⑤ Area = _____

Perimeter = _____

7 cm | 4 cm
23 cm

⑥ Area = _____

Perimeter = _____

20 cm | 24 cm
24 cm

⑦ Area = _____

Perimeter = _____

4 cm | 6 cm
16 cm

⑧ Area = _____

Perimeter = _____

30 cm | 45 cm
37 cm

⑨ Area = _____

Perimeter = _____

31 cm | 37 cm
49 cm

Name: _____

Score:

①
Area = _____
Perimeter = _____

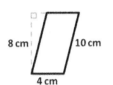

8 cm | 10 cm
4 cm

②
Area = _____
Perimeter = _____

5 cm | 6 cm
15 cm

③
Area = _____
Perimeter = _____

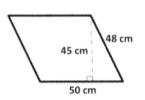

36 cm
47 cm
23 cm

④
Area = _____
Perimeter = _____

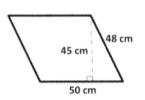

48 cm
45 cm
50 cm

⑤
Area = _____
Perimeter = _____

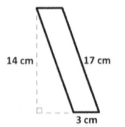

14 cm | 17 cm
3 cm

⑥
Area = _____
Perimeter = _____

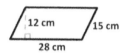

12 cm | 15 cm
28 cm

⑦
Area = _____
Perimeter = _____

7 cm | 6 cm
2 cm

⑧
Area = _____
Perimeter = _____

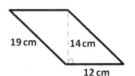

19 cm | 14 cm
12 cm

⑨
Area = _____
Perimeter = _____

45 cm | 55 cm
30 cm

Name: _____

Score:

Trapezoids

Perimeter

Add all the sides together.

$$Perimeter = a + b + c + d$$

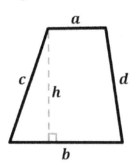

Area

Add both bases,
divide by 2,
then multiply the height.

$$Area = \frac{a + b}{2} \times h$$

---

①

Area = _____

Perimeter = _____

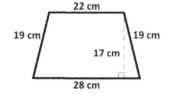

22 cm

19 cm   19 cm

17 cm

28 cm

---

②

Area = _____

Perimeter = _____

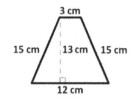

3 cm

15 cm   13 cm   15 cm

12 cm

---

③

Area = _____

Perimeter = _____

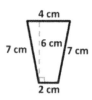

4 cm

7 cm   6 cm   7 cm

2 cm

---

④

Area = _____

Perimeter = _____

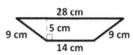

28 cm

9 cm   5 cm   9 cm

14 cm

---

⑤

Area = _____

Perimeter = _____

16 cm

15 cm   11 cm   13 cm

24 cm

---

⑥

Area = _____

Perimeter = _____

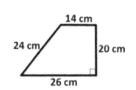

14 cm

24 cm   20 cm

26 cm

Day 14

Trapezoids

Name: _____

Score:

① Area = _____
Perimeter = _____

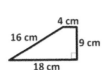

4 cm
16 cm
9 cm
18 cm

② Area = _____
Perimeter = _____

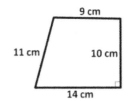

17 cm
9 cm | 7 cm | 10 cm
13 cm

③ Area = _____
Perimeter = _____

9 cm
11 cm | 10 cm
14 cm

④ Area = _____
Perimeter = _____

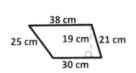

38 cm
25 cm | 19 cm | 21 cm
30 cm

⑤ Area = _____
Perimeter = _____

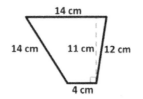

14 cm
14 cm | 11 cm | 12 cm
4 cm

⑥ Area = _____
Perimeter = _____

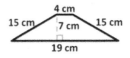

4 cm
15 cm | 7 cm | 15 cm
19 cm

⑦ Area = _____
Perimeter = _____

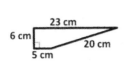

23 cm
6 cm
20 cm
5 cm

⑧ Area = _____
Perimeter = _____

33 cm
27 cm | 20 cm | 29 cm
5 cm

⑨ Area = _____
Perimeter = _____

21 cm
11 cm | 10 cm | 17 cm
28 cm

© Libro Studio LLC 2020

Name: _____

Score:

① Area = _____
Perimeter = _____

22 cm
15 cm | 12 cm | 15 cm
9 cm

② Area = _____
Perimeter = _____

28 cm
12 cm | 15 cm
22 cm

③ Area = _____
Perimeter = _____

11 cm
9 cm | 4 cm | 6cm
15 cm

④ Area = _____
Perimeter = _____

22 cm
14 cm | 12 cm | 14 cm
18 cm

⑤ Area = _____
Perimeter = _____

18 cm
3 cm | 2 cm | 3 cm
15 cm

⑥ Area = _____
Perimeter = _____

11 cm
6 cm | 3 cm | 6 cm
1 cm

⑦ Area = _____
Perimeter = _____

10 cm
11 cm | 7 cm | 12 cm
27 cm

⑧ Area = _____
Perimeter = _____

16 cm
9 cm | 7 cm | 13 cm
3 cm

⑨ Area = _____
Perimeter = _____

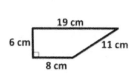

19 cm
6 cm | 11 cm
8 cm

Name: _____

Score:

Circles

Circumference

2 times pi times the radius.

$$C = 2 \times \pi \times r$$

Or

Pi times the diameter.

$$C = \pi \times d$$

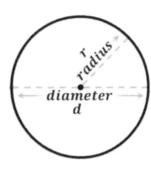

Area

Pi times the radius squared.

$$Area = \pi \times r^2$$

(π is about 3.14)

Have 3.14 represent π when calculating each problem. Round each answer to the nearest hundredth.

① Area = _____
Circumference = _____

② Area = _____
Circumference = _____

③ Area = _____
Circumference = _____

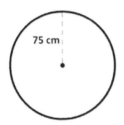

75 cm

36 cm

44 cm

④ Area = _____
Circumference = _____

⑤ Area = _____
Circumference = _____

⑥ Area = _____
Circumference = _____

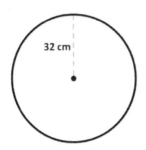

32 cm

85 cm

26 cm

Name: _____

Score:

Have 3.14 represent π when calculating each problem. Round each answer to the nearest hundredth.

① Area = _____
Circumference = _____

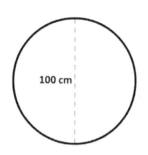

100 cm

② Area = _____
Circumference = _____

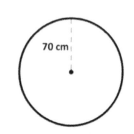

70 cm

③ Area = _____
Circumference = _____

12 cm

④ Area = _____
Circumference = _____

6 cm

⑤ Area = _____
Circumference = _____

8 cm

⑥ Area = _____
Circumference = _____

5 cm

⑦ Area = _____
Circumference = _____

425 cm

⑧ Area = _____
Circumference = _____

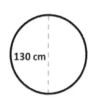

130 cm

⑨ Area = _____
Circumference = _____

1 cm

Day 18
Circles

Name: _____

Score:

Have 3.14 represent π when calculating each problem. Round each answer to the nearest hundredth.

①
Area = _____
Circumference = _____

17 cm

②
Area = _____
Circumference = _____

9 cm

③
Area = _____
Circumference = _____

120 cm

④
Area = _____
Circumference = _____

8 cm

⑤
Area = _____
Circumference = _____

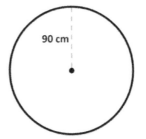

90 cm

⑥
Area = _____
Circumference = _____

9 cm

⑦
Area = _____
Circumference = _____

71 cm

⑧
Area = _____
Circumference = _____

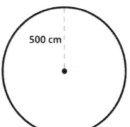

500 cm

⑨
Area = _____
Circumference = _____

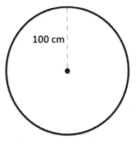

100 cm

Have 3.14 represent π when calculating each problem. Round each answer to the nearest hundredth.

① Area = _____
Circumference = _____

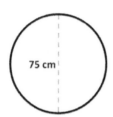

75 cm

② Area = _____
Circumference = _____

50 cm

③ Area = _____
Circumference = _____

14 cm

④ Area = _____
Circumference = _____

33 cm

⑤ Area = _____
Circumference = _____

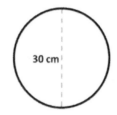

30 cm

⑥ Area = _____
Circumference = _____

85 cm

⑦ Area = _____
Circumference = _____

240 cm

⑧ Area = _____
Circumference = _____

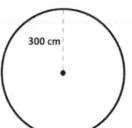

300 cm

⑨ Area = _____
Circumference = _____

21 cm

Name: _____

Have 3.14 represent π when calculating each problem. Round each answer to the nearest hundredth.

① Area = _____
Perimeter = _____

7 cm
7 cm

② Area = _____
Circumference = _____

2 cm

③ Area = _____
Perimeter = _____

43 cm   20 cm
31 cm

④ Area = _____
Perimeter = _____

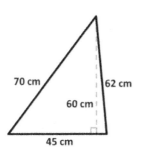

70 cm   62 cm
60 cm
45 cm

⑤ Area = _____
Perimeter = _____

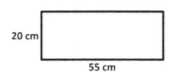

20 cm
55 cm

⑥ Area = _____
Perimeter = _____

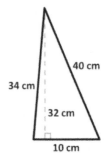

40 cm
34 cm
32 cm
10 cm

⑦ Area = _____
Perimeter = _____

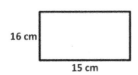

16 cm
15 cm

⑧ Area = _____
Perimeter = _____

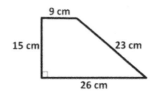

9 cm
15 cm   23 cm
26 cm

⑨ Area = _____
Circumference = _____

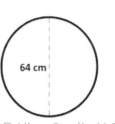

64 cm

Name: _____

Score:

Have 3.14 represent π when calculating each problem. Round each answer to the nearest hundredth.

①
Area = _____
Circumference = _____

50 cm

②
Area = _____
Perimeter = _____

8 cm

10 cm

③
Area = _____
Perimeter = _____

16 cm   25 cm
20 cm
15 cm

④
Area = _____
Perimeter = _____

17 cm   19 cm
12 cm

⑤
Area = _____
Circumference = _____

15 cm

⑥
Area = _____
Perimeter = _____

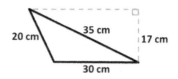
35 cm
20 cm   17 cm
30 cm

⑦
Area = _____
Perimeter = _____

18 cm
30 cm

⑧
Area = _____
Perimeter = _____

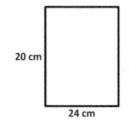
20 cm
24 cm

⑨
Area = _____
Perimeter = _____

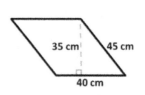
35 cm   45 cm
40 cm

Name: _____

Have 3.14 represent π when calculating each problem. Round each answer to the nearest hundredth.

① Area = _____
Circumference = _____

1 cm

② Area = _____
Perimeter = _____

20 cm   60 cm
55 cm

③ Area = _____
Perimeter = _____

25 cm
9 cm

④ Area = _____
Perimeter = _____

28 cm
14 cm 12 cm 14 cm
36 cm

⑤ Area = _____
Perimeter = _____

27 cm   30 cm
20 cm

⑥ Area = _____
Perimeter = _____

6 cm
2 cm

⑦ Area = _____
Circumference = _____

3 cm

⑧ Area = _____
Perimeter = _____

9 cm
42 cm

⑨ Area = _____
Perimeter = _____

34 cm   20 cm
22 cm
24 cm

Name: _____

Score:

Have 3.14 represent π when calculating each problem. Round each answer to the nearest hundredth.

① Area = _____
Perimeter = _____

2 cm ▭ 3 cm

② Area = _____
Perimeter = _____

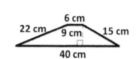
22 cm 6 cm 9 cm 15 cm 40 cm

③ Area = _____
Perimeter = _____

15 cm 17 cm 25 cm

④ Area = _____
Perimeter = _____

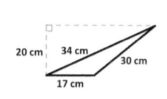
20 cm 34 cm 30 cm 17 cm

⑤ Area = _____
Circumference = _____

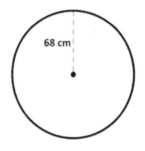
68 cm

⑥ Area = _____
Perimeter = _____

7 cm ▭ 23 cm

⑦ Area = _____
Perimeter = _____

39 cm 24 cm

⑧ Area = _____
Perimeter = _____

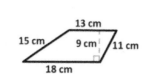
13 cm 15 cm 9 cm 11 cm 18 cm

⑨ Area = _____
Circumference = _____

94 cm

Day 24
Mixed Review

Name: _____

Score:

Have 3.14 represent π when calculating each problem. Round each answer to the nearest hundredth.

① Area = _____
Perimeter = _____

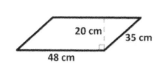
20 cm · 35 cm
48 cm

② Area = _____
Perimeter = _____

32 cm
29 cm

③ Area = _____
Circumference = _____

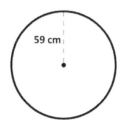
59 cm

④ Area = _____
Perimeter = _____

11 cm
20 cm

⑤ Area = _____
Circumference = _____

300 cm

⑥ Area = _____
Perimeter = _____

55 cm
35 cm

⑦ Area = _____
Perimeter = _____

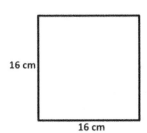
16 cm
16 cm

⑧ Area = _____
Circumference = _____

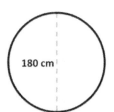
180 cm

⑨ Area = _____
Perimeter = _____

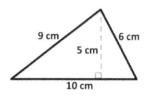
9 cm   6 cm
5 cm
10 cm

Name: _____

Score:

Have 3.14 represent π when calculating each problem. Round each answer to the nearest hundredth.

① Area = _____

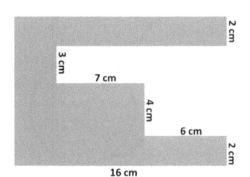

② Area = _____

③ Area = _____

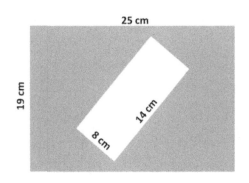

④ Area = _____

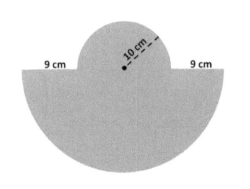

⑤ Area = _____

⑥ Area = _____

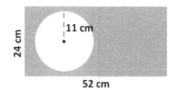

Day 26
Multi-Step Problems

Name: _____

Score:

① Area = _____

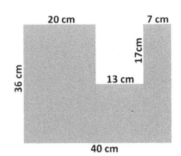

20 cm | 7 cm
17 cm
36 cm
13 cm
40 cm

② Area = _____

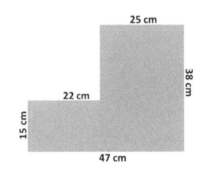

25 cm
38 cm
22 cm
15 cm
47 cm

③ Area = _____

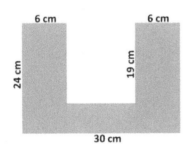

6 cm | 6 cm
24 cm | 19 cm
30 cm

④ Area = _____

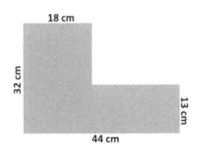

18 cm
32 cm
13 cm
44 cm

⑤ Area = _____

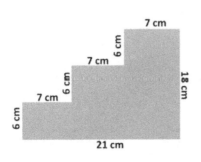

7 cm
6 cm
7 cm
6 cm
7 cm
18 cm
6 cm
21 cm

⑥ Area = _____

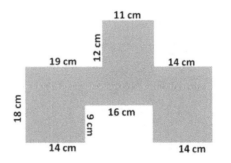

11 cm
12 cm
19 cm | 14 cm
18 cm | 16 cm
9 cm
14 cm | 14 cm

Day 27
Multi-Step Problems

Name: _____

Score:

Have 3.14 represent π when calculating each problem. Round each answer to the nearest hundredth.

①

Area = _____

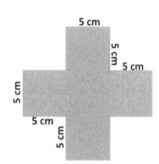

5 cm
5 cm
5 cm
5 cm
5 cm
5 cm
5 cm

②

Area = _____

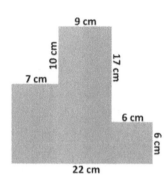

9 cm
10 cm
17 cm
7 cm
6 cm
6 cm
22 cm

③

Area = _____

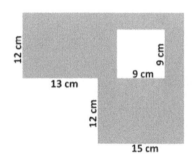

12 cm
9 cm
9 cm
13 cm
12 cm
15 cm

④

Area = _____

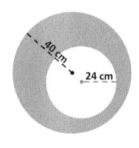

40 cm
24 cm

⑤

Area = _____

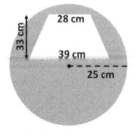

28 cm
33 cm
39 cm
25 cm

⑥

Area = _____

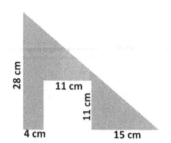

28 cm
11 cm
11 cm
4 cm
15 cm

Day 28
Multi-Step Problems

Name: _____

Score:

Have 3.14 represent π when calculating each problem. Round each answer to the nearest hundredth.

① Area = _____

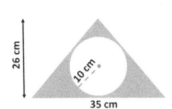

② Area = _____

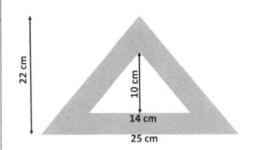

③ Area = _____

④ Area = _____

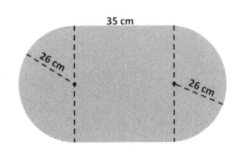

⑤ Area = _____

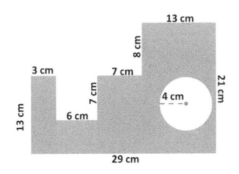

⑥ Area = _____

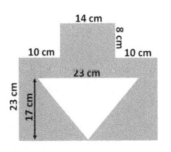

Day 29

Multi-Step Problems

Name: _____

Score:

Have 3.14 represent π when calculating each problem. Round each answer to the nearest hundredth.

① Area = _____

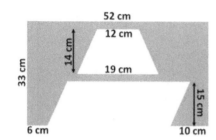

52 cm
12 cm
14 cm
19 cm
33 cm
15 cm
6 cm
10 cm

② Area = _____

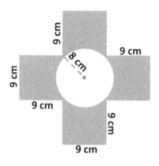

9 cm
9 cm
9 cm
8 cm
9 cm
9 cm
9 cm

③ Area = _____

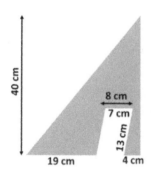

40 cm
8 cm
7 cm
13 cm
19 cm
4 cm

④ Area = _____

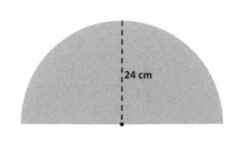

24 cm

⑤ Area = _____

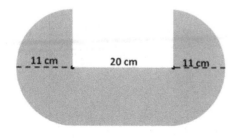

11 cm
20 cm
11 cm

⑥ Area = _____

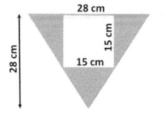

28 cm
15 cm
28 cm
15 cm

Name: _____

Score:

Prisms

Volume of a Prism

Area of the base
times the height.

$Volume = Base \times height$

$V = B \times h$

What is the base?

Rectangular prisms have
rectangular bases.

Triangular prisms have
triangular bases

Parallelepipeds have
parallelogram bases

Trapezoidal prisms have
trapezoid bases.

---

① Volume = _____

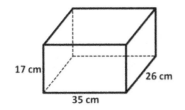

17 cm, 26 cm, 35 cm

② Volume = _____

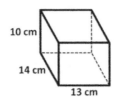

10 cm, 14 cm, 13 cm

③ Volume = _____

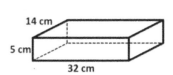

14 cm, 5 cm, 32 cm

---

④ Volume = _____

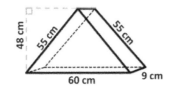

48 cm, 55 cm, 55 cm, 60 cm, 9 cm

⑤ Volume = _____

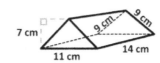

7 cm, 9 cm, 9 cm, 11 cm, 14 cm

⑥ Volume = _____

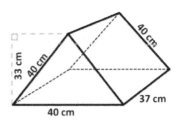

40 cm, 33 cm, 40 cm, 37 cm, 40 cm

Day 31
Prisms

① Volume = _____

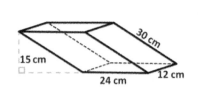

30 cm
15 cm
12 cm
24 cm

② Volume = _____

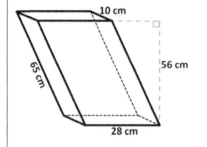

10 cm
65 cm
56 cm
28 cm

③ Volume = _____

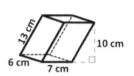

13 cm
10 cm
6 cm
7 cm

④ Volume = _____

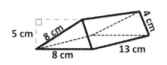

5 cm
8 cm
8 cm
4 cm
13 cm

⑤ Volume = _____

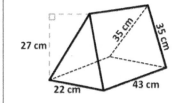

27 cm
35 cm
35 cm
22 cm
43 cm

⑥ Volume = _____

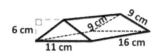

6 cm
9 cm
9 cm
11 cm
16 cm

⑦ Volume = _____

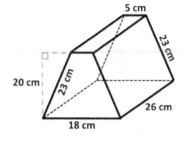

5 cm
23 cm
20 cm
23 cm
26 cm
18 cm

⑧ Volume = _____

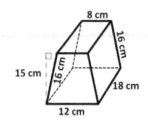

8 cm
16 cm
15 cm
16 cm
18 cm
12 cm

⑨ Volume = _____

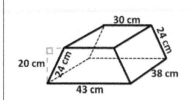

30 cm
24 cm
20 cm
24 cm
38 cm
43 cm

Name: _____

① Volume = _____

4 cm
5 cm
7 cm

② Volume = _____

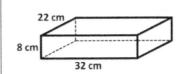

22 cm
8 cm
32 cm

③ Volume = _____

3 cm
2 cm
2 cm

④ Volume = _____

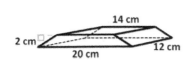

14 cm
2 cm
20 cm
12 cm

⑤ Volume = _____

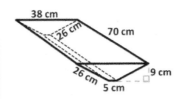

38 cm
26 cm
70 cm
26 cm
9 cm
5 cm

⑥ Volume = _____

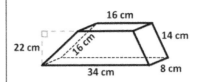

16 cm
14 cm
22 cm
16 cm
34 cm
8 cm

⑦ Volume = _____

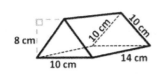

10 cm
10 cm
8 cm
10 cm
14 cm

⑧ Volume = _____

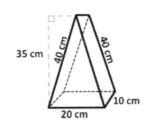

35 cm
40 cm
40 cm
10 cm
20 cm

⑨ Volume = _____

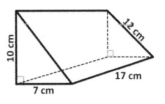

12 cm
10 cm
17 cm
7 cm

Day 33
Prisms

Name: _____

① Volume = _____

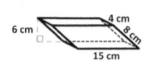

6 cm   4 cm
        8 cm
    15 cm

② Volume = _____

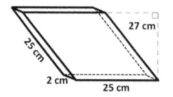

27 cm
25 cm
2 cm   25 cm

③ Volume = _____

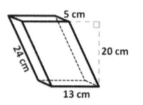

5 cm
24 cm   20 cm
    13 cm

④ Volume = _____

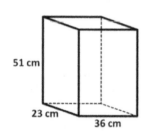

51 cm
23 cm
    36 cm

⑤ Volume = _____

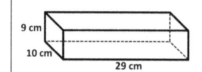

9 cm
10 cm
    29 cm

⑥ Volume = _____

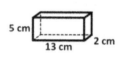

5 cm
    2 cm
13 cm

⑦ Volume = _____

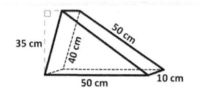

35 cm   50 cm
    40 cm
    50 cm   10 cm

⑧ Volume = _____

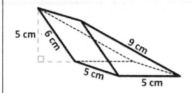

5 cm   6 cm   9 cm
    5 cm   5 cm

⑨ Volume = _____

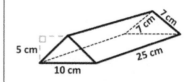

7 cm
7 cm
5 cm
    10 cm   25 cm

Day 34
Prisms

Name: _____

Score:

① Volume = _____

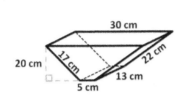

30 cm
20 cm
17 cm
13 cm
5 cm
22 cm

② Volume = _____

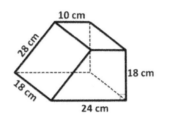

10 cm
28 cm
18 cm
18 cm
24 cm

③ Volume = _____

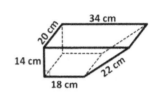

34 cm
20 cm
14 cm
18 cm
22 cm

④ Volume = _____

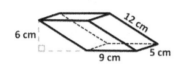

12 cm
6 cm
9 cm
5 cm

⑤ Volume = _____

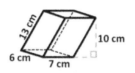

13 cm
6 cm
7 cm
10 cm

⑥ Volume = _____

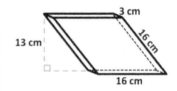

3 cm
13 cm
16 cm
16 cm

⑦ Volume = _____

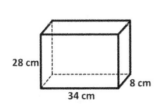

28 cm
34 cm
8 cm

⑧ Volume = _____

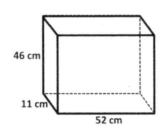

46 cm
11 cm
52 cm

⑨ Volume = _____

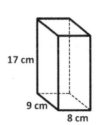

17 cm
9 cm
8 cm

Name: _____

Score:

Cylinders

Volume of a Cylinder

Area of the base times the height.

$Volume = Base \times height$

$V = B \times h$

What is the base?

Cylinders have circular bases.

Do you remember how to find the area of a circle?

Have 3.14 represent π when calculating each problem. Round each answer to the nearest hundredth.

① Volume = _____

② Area = _____

③ Volume = _____

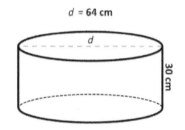

d = 64 cm

d

30 cm

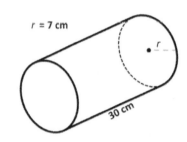

r = 7 cm

r

30 cm

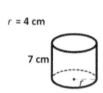

r = 4 cm

7 cm

④ Volume = _____

⑤ Volume = _____

⑥ Volume = _____

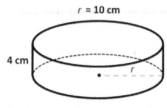

r = 10 cm

4 cm

r

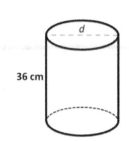

d = 20 cm

d

36 cm

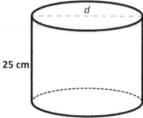

d = 25 cm

d

25 cm

Day 36

Cylinders

Have 3.14 represent π when calculating each problem. Round each answer to the nearest hundredth.

① Volume = _____

$r = 3$ cm

9 cm

② Volume = _____

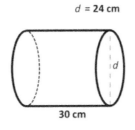

$d = 24$ cm

d

30 cm

③ Volume = _____

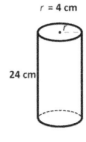

$r = 4$ cm

24 cm

④ Volume = _____

$r = 15$ cm

23 cm

⑤ Volume = _____

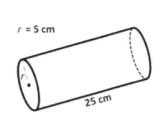

$r = 5$ cm

25 cm

⑥ Volume = _____

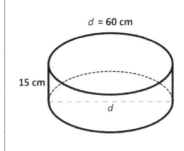

$d = 60$ cm

15 cm

d

⑦ Volume = _____

$r = 7$ cm

r

5 cm

⑧ Volume = _____

$d = 3$ cm

26 cm

d

⑨ Volume = _____

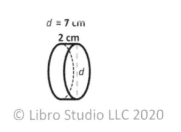

$d = 7$ cm

2 cm

d

© Libro Studio LLC 2020

Name: _____

Score:

Have 3.14 represent π when calculating each problem. Round each answer to the nearest hundredth.

①

Volume = _____

r = 5 cm

10 cm

②

Volume = _____

r = 8 cm

14 cm

r

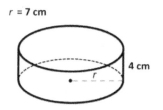

③

Volume = _____

r = 7 cm

4 cm

r

④

Volume = _____

d = 20 cm

d

12 cm

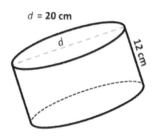

⑤

Volume = _____

4 cm

r = 4 cm

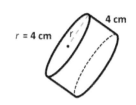

⑥

Volume = _____

r = 6 cm

r

14 cm

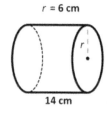

⑦

Volume = _____

r = 15 cm

r

9 cm

⑧

Volume = _____

d = 30 cm

d

25 cm

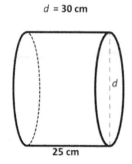

⑨

Volume = _____

d = 12 cm

16 cm

d

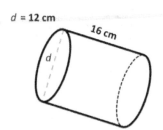

Name: _____

Cones

Area

Pie times *r* squared times one third of the height.

$$Area = \pi \times r^2 \times \frac{height}{3}$$

$$A = \pi r^2 \frac{h}{3}$$

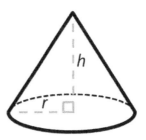

Have 3.14 represent π when calculating each problem. Round each answer to the nearest hundredth.

① Volume = _____

h = 110 cm
r = 54 cm

② Volume = _____

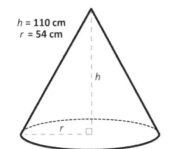

h = 50 cm
r = 15 cm

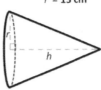

③ Volume = _____

h = 8 cm
r = 9 cm

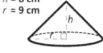

④ Volume = _____

h = 30 cm
r = 20 cm

⑤ Volume = _____

h = 6 cm
r = 10 cm

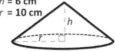

⑥ Volume = _____

h = 27 cm
r = 15 cm

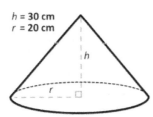

Day 39
Cones

Name: _____

Score:

Have 3.14 represent π when calculating each problem. Round each answer to the nearest hundredth.

① Volume = _____

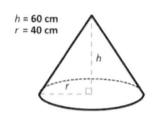

h = 60 cm
r = 40 cm

② Volume = _____

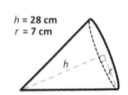

h = 28 cm
r = 7 cm

③ Volume = _____

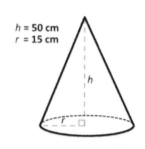

h = 50 cm
r = 15 cm

④ Volume = _____

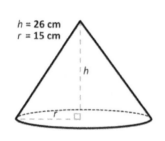

h = 26 cm
r = 15 cm

⑤ Volume = _____

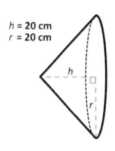

h = 20 cm
r = 20 cm

⑥ Volume = _____

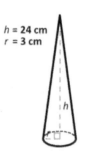

h = 24 cm
r = 3 cm

⑦ Volume = _____

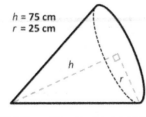

h = 75 cm
r = 25 cm

⑧ Volume = _____

h = 8 cm
r = 3 cm

⑨ Volume = _____

h = 22 cm
r = 11 cm

Name: _____

Score:

Have 3.14 represent π when calculating each problem. Round each answer to the nearest hundredth.

① Volume = _____

h = 8 cm
r = 20 cm

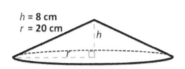

② Volume = _____

h = 25 cm
r = 11 cm

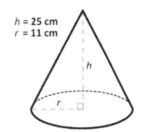

③ Volume = _____

h = 100 cm
r = 20 cm

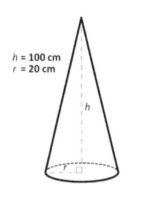

④ Volume = _____

h = 17 cm
r = 12 cm

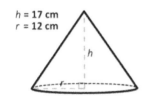

⑤ Volume = _____

h = 36 cm
r = 25 cm

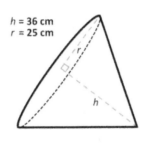

⑥ Volume = _____

h = 15 cm
r = 8 cm

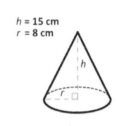

⑦ Volume = _____

h = 65 cm
r = 10 cm

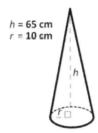

⑧ Volume = _____

h = 100 cm
r = 35 cm

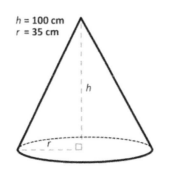

⑨ Volume = _____

h = 13 cm
r = 8 cm

Name: _____

Score:

Have 3.14 represent π when calculating each problem. Round each answer to the nearest hundredth.

① Volume = _____

h = 45 cm
r = 20 cm

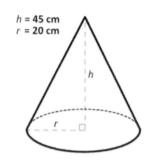

② Volume = _____

h = 40 cm
r = 24 cm

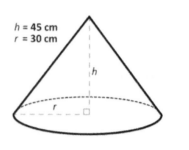

③ Volume = _____

h = 45 cm
r = 30 cm

④ Volume = _____

h = 14 cm
r = 12 cm

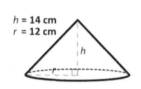

⑤ Volume = _____

h = 40 cm
r = 10 cm

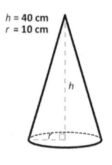

⑥ Volume = _____

h = 35 cm
r = 20 cm

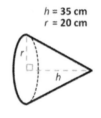

⑦ Volume = _____

h = 62 cm
r = 25 cm

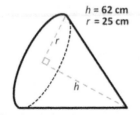

⑧ Volume = _____

h = 21 cm
r = 50 cm

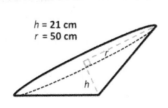

⑨ Volume = _____

h = 20 cm
r = 4 cm

Name: _____

Score:

Pyramids

Volume

Multiply the <u>area of the base</u> by the <u>height</u>, then <u>divide by three</u>.

$$Volume = \frac{Base \times height}{3}$$

$$\boldsymbol{Volume = \frac{B \times h}{3}}$$

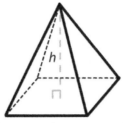

Rectangular Pyramids have rectangle bases.

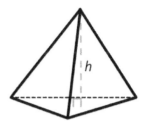

Triangular Pyramids have triangle bases.

---

① Volume = _____

h = 20 cm

16 cm

16 cm

② Volume = _____

h = 72 cm

17 cm

44 cm

③ Volume = _____

h = 5 cm

3 cm

2 cm

---

④ Volume = _____

h = 40 cm

30 cm

10 cm

⑤ Volume = _____

h = 30 cm

10 cm

20 cm

⑥ Volume = _____

h = 6 cm

12 cm

8 cm

Name: _____

Score:

① Volume = _____

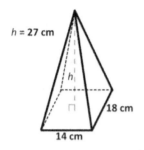

h = 27 cm
h
18 cm
14 cm

② Volume = _____

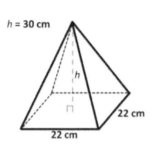

h = 30 cm
h
22 cm
22 cm

③ Volume = _____

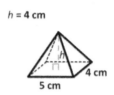

h = 4 cm
h
4 cm
5 cm

④ Volume = _____

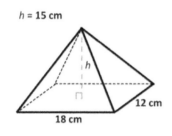

h = 15 cm
h
12 cm
18 cm

⑤ Volume = _____

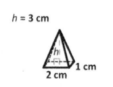

h = 3 cm
h
1 cm
2 cm

⑥ Volume = _____

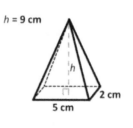

h = 9 cm
h
2 cm
5 cm

⑦ Volume = _____

h = 48 cm
h
12 cm
34 cm

⑧ Volume = _____

h = 10 cm
h
10 cm
14 cm

⑨ Volume = _____

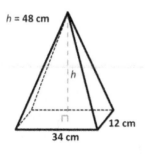

h = 40 cm
h
27 cm
15 cm

Day 44
Triangular Pyramids

Name: _____

Score:

① Volume = _____

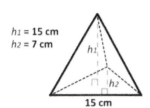

h_1 = 15 cm
h_2 = 7 cm
h_1
h_2
15 cm

② Volume = _____

h_1 = 32 cm
h_2 = 11 cm
h_1
h_2
25 cm

③ Volume = _____

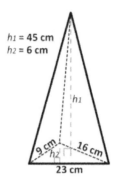

h_1 = 45 cm
h_2 = 6 cm
h_1
9 cm   16 cm
h_2
23 cm

④ Volume = _____

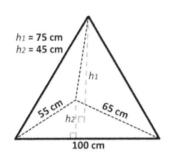

h_1 = 75 cm
h_2 = 45 cm
h_1
55 cm   65 cm
h_2
100 cm

⑤ Volume = _____

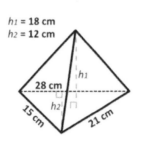

h_1 = 18 cm
h_2 = 12 cm
h_1
28 cm
h_2
15 cm   21 cm

⑥ Volume = _____

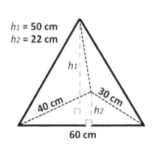

h_1 = 50 cm
h_2 = 22 cm
h_1
40 cm   30 cm
h_2
60 cm

⑦ Volume = _____

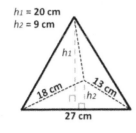

h_1 = 20 cm
h_2 = 9 cm
h_1
18 cm   13 cm
h_2
27 cm

⑧ Volume = _____

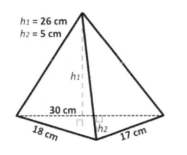

h_1 = 26 cm
h_2 = 5 cm
h_1
30 cm
h_2
18 cm   17 cm

⑨ Volume = _____

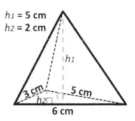

h_1 = 5 cm
h_2 = 2 cm
h_1
3 cm   5 cm
h_2
6 cm

Day 45
Triangular Pyramids

Name: _____

Score:

① Volume = _____

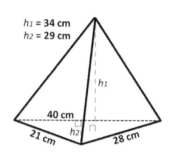

$h_1 = 34$ cm
$h_2 = 29$ cm
h_1
40 cm
21 cm
h_2
28 cm

② Volume = _____

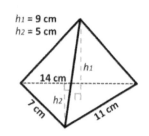

$h_1 = 9$ cm
$h_2 = 5$ cm
h_1
14 cm
h_2
7 cm
11 cm

③ Volume = _____

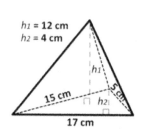

$h_1 = 12$ cm
$h_2 = 4$ cm
h_1
15 cm
5 cm
h_2
17 cm

④ Volume = _____

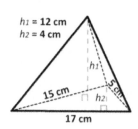

$h_1 = 12$ cm
$h_2 = 4$ cm
h_1
15 cm
5 cm
h_2
17 cm

⑤ Volume = _____

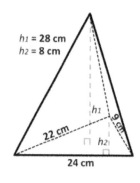

$h_1 = 28$ cm
$h_2 = 8$ cm
h_1
22 cm
9 cm
h_2
24 cm

⑥ Volume = _____

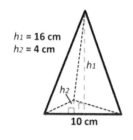

$h_1 = 16$ cm
$h_2 = 4$ cm
h_1
h_2
10 cm

⑦ Volume = _____

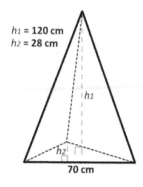

$h_1 = 120$ cm
$h_2 = 28$ cm
h_1
h_2
70 cm

⑧ Volume = _____

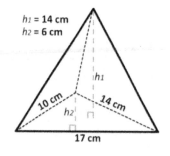

$h_1 = 14$ cm
$h_2 = 6$ cm
h_1
10 cm
14 cm
h_2
17 cm

⑨ Volume = _____

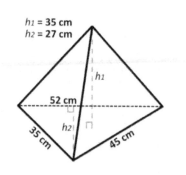

$h_1 = 35$ cm
$h_2 = 27$ cm
h_1
52 cm
h_2
35 cm
45 cm

Name: _____

Score:

① Volume = _____

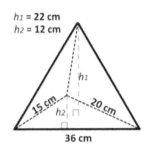

h_1 = 22 cm
h_2 = 12 cm
h_1
15 cm   20 cm
h_2
36 cm

② Volume = _____

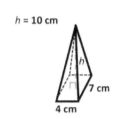

h = 10 cm
h
7 cm
4 cm

③ Volume = _____

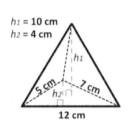

h_1 = 10 cm
h_2 = 4 cm
h_1
5 cm   7 cm
h_2
12 cm

④ Volume = _____

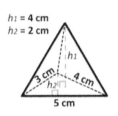

h_1 = 4 cm
h_2 = 2 cm
h_1
3 cm   4 cm
h_2
5 cm

⑤ Volume = _____

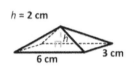

h = 2 cm
h
6 cm   3 cm

⑥ Volume = _____

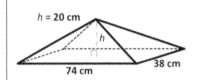

h = 20 cm
h
74 cm   38 cm

⑦ Volume = _____

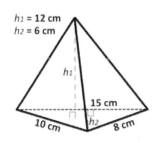

h_1 = 12 cm
h_2 = 6 cm
h_1
15 cm
10 cm h_2 8 cm

⑧ Volume = _____

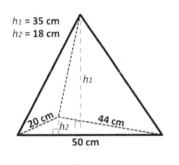

h_1 = 35 cm
h_2 = 18 cm
h_1
20 cm   44 cm
h_2
50 cm

⑨ Volume = _____

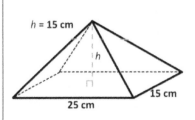

h = 15 cm
h
15 cm
25 cm

Day 47
Pyramids Mixed Review

Name: _____

Score:

---

① Volume = _____

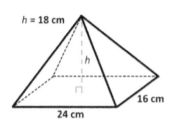

h = 18 cm

h

16 cm

24 cm

---

② Volume = _____

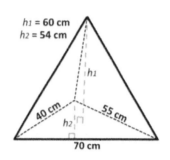

h1 = 60 cm
h2 = 54 cm

h1

40 cm   55 cm

h2

70 cm

---

③ Volume = _____

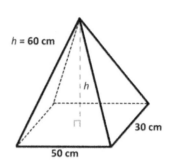

h = 60 cm

h

30 cm

50 cm

---

④ Volume = _____

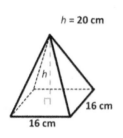

h = 20 cm

h

16 cm

16 cm

---

⑤ Volume = _____

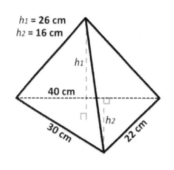

h1 = 26 cm
h2 = 16 cm

h1

40 cm

30 cm   h2   22 cm

---

⑥ Volume = _____

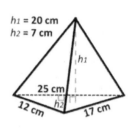

h1 = 20 cm
h2 = 7 cm

h1

25 cm

12 cm   h2   17 cm

---

⑦ Volume = _____

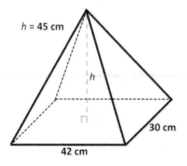

h = 45 cm

h

30 cm

42 cm

---

⑧ Volume = _____

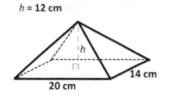

h = 12 cm

h

20 cm   14 cm

---

⑨ Volume = _____

h1 = 12 cm
h2 = 9 cm

h1

15 cm   25 cm

h2

35 cm

Name: _____

Score:

Sphere

Volume

Four thirds, times pie, times r cubed.

$Volume = \dfrac{4}{3} \times \pi \times r^3$

$V = \dfrac{4}{3}\pi r^3$

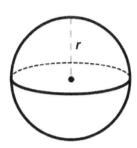

(π is about 3.14)

Have 3.14 represent π when calculating each problem. Round each answer to the nearest hundredth.

① Volume = _____

② Volume = _____

③ Volume = _____

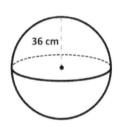

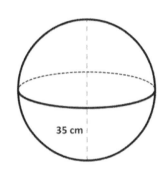

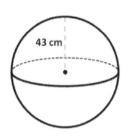

④ Volume = _____

⑤ Volume = _____

⑥ Volume = _____

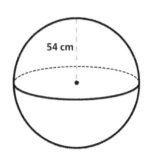

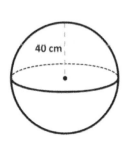

Day 49
Spheres

Name: _____

Score:

Have 3.14 represent π when calculating each problem. Round each answer to the nearest hundredth.

① Volume = _____

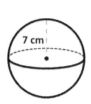

7 cm

② Volume = _____

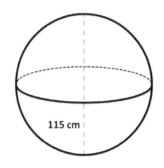

115 cm

③ Volume = _____

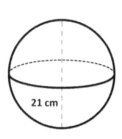

21 cm

④ Volume = _____

4 cm

⑤ Volume = _____

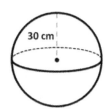

30 cm

⑥ Volume = _____

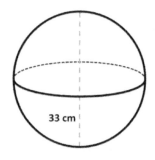

33 cm

⑦ Volume = _____

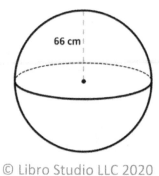

66 cm

⑧ Volume = _____

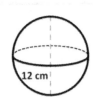

12 cm

⑨ Volume = _____

3 cm

Day 50
Spheres

Name: _____

Score:

Have 3.14 represent π when calculating each problem. Round each answer to the nearest hundredth.

① Volume = _____

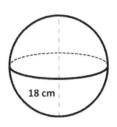
18 cm

② Volume = _____

1 cm

③ Volume = _____

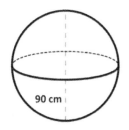
90 cm

④ Volume = _____

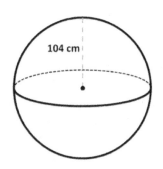
104 cm

⑤ Volume = _____

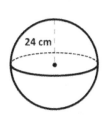
24 cm

⑥ Volume = _____

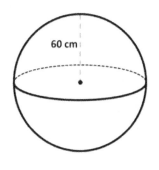
60 cm

⑦ Volume = _____

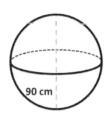
90 cm

⑧ Volume = _____

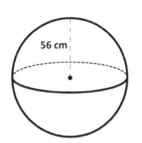
56 cm

⑨ Volume = _____

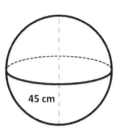
45 cm

Name: _____

Score:

Have 3.14 represent π when calculating each problem. Round each answer to the nearest hundredth.

① Volume = _____

r = 12 cm

7 cm

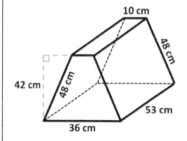

② Volume = _____

10 cm
48 cm
42 cm
48 cm
53 cm
36 cm

③ Volume = _____

h = 6 cm
h
5 cm
8 cm

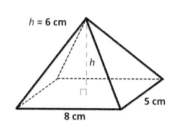

④ Volume = _____

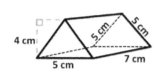

4 cm
5 cm
5 cm
5 cm
7 cm

⑤ Volume = _____

6 cm

⑥ Volume = _____

8 cm
13 cm
17 cm

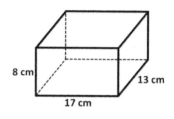

⑦ Volume = _____

5 cm
12 cm
12 cm
6 cm
20 cm

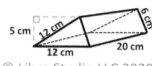

⑧ Volume = _____

h = 32 cm
r = 16 cm
r
h

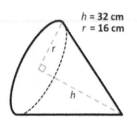

⑨ Volume = _____

1 cm
5 cm
6 cm
3 cm

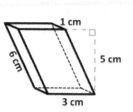

Day 52
Volume Mixed Review

Name: _____

Score:

Have 3.14 represent π when calculating each problem. Round each answer to the nearest hundredth.

① Volume = _____

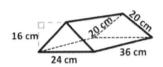

16 cm
20 cm
20 cm
24 cm
36 cm

② Volume = _____

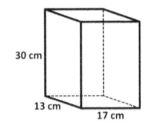

30 cm
13 cm
17 cm

③ Volume = _____

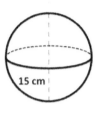

15 cm

④ Volume = _____

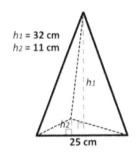

h_1 = 32 cm
h_2 = 11 cm
h_1
h_2
25 cm

⑤ Volume = _____

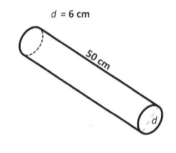

d = 6 cm
50 cm
d

⑥ Volume = _____

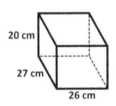

20 cm
27 cm
26 cm

⑦ Volume = _____

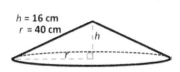

h = 16 cm
r = 40 cm
h
r

⑧ Volume = _____

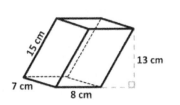

15 cm
13 cm
7 cm
8 cm

⑨ Volume = _____

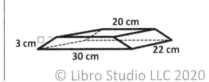

20 cm
3 cm
30 cm
22 cm

Day 53
Volume Mixed Review

Name: _____

Score:

Have 3.14 represent π when calculating each problem. Round each answer to the nearest hundredth.

① Volume = _____

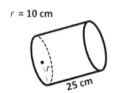

20 cm
12 cm
37 cm
12 cm
5 cm
2 cm

② Volume = _____

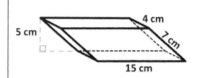

r = 10 cm
25 cm

③ Volume = _____

4 cm
5 cm
7 cm
15 cm

④ Volume = _____

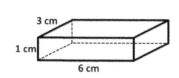

3 cm
1 cm
6 cm

⑤ Volume = _____

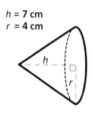

h = 7 cm
r = 4 cm
h

⑥ Volume = _____

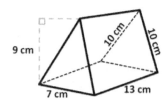

9 cm
10 cm
10 cm
7 cm
13 cm

⑦ Volume = _____

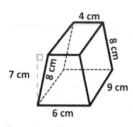

4 cm
8 cm
7 cm
8 cm
9 cm
6 cm

⑧ Volume = _____

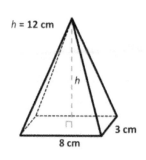

h = 12 cm
h
3 cm
8 cm

⑨ Volume = _____

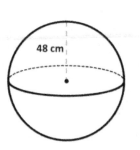

48 cm

Day 54
Volume Mixed Review

Name: _____

Score:

Have 3.14 represent π when calculating each problem. Round each answer to the nearest hundredth.

① Volume = _____

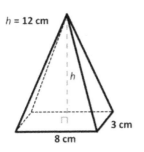

h = 12 cm
3 cm
8 cm

② Volume = _____

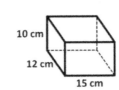

10 cm
12 cm
15 cm

③ Volume = _____

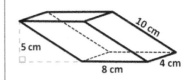

10 cm
5 cm
8 cm
4 cm

④ Volume = _____

25 cm

⑤ Volume = _____

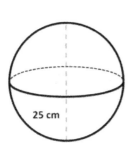

19 cm
14 cm
19 cm
16 cm
23 cm

⑥ Volume = _____

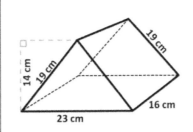

h = 26 cm
r = 14 cm
h
r

⑦ Volume = _____

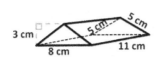

3 cm
5 cm
5 cm
8 cm
11 cm

⑧ Volume = _____

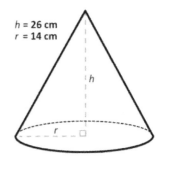

8 cm
7 cm
11 cm
8 cm
17 cm
4 cm

⑨ Volume = _____

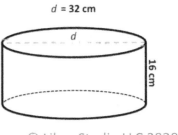

d = 32 cm
d
16 cm

© Libro Studio LLC 2020

Name: _____

Score:

Have 3.14 represent π when calculating each problem. Round each answer to the nearest hundredth.

① Volume = _____

30 cm
10 cm
70 cm
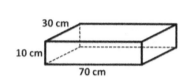

② Volume = _____

11 cm
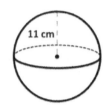

③ Volume = _____

$r = 14$ cm
r
60 cm
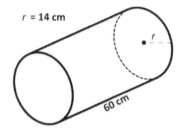

④ Volume = _____

15 cm
12 cm
12 cm
10 cm
17 cm
22 cm
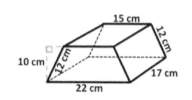

⑤ Volume = _____

$h = 13$ cm
$r = 15$ cm
h
r
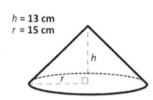

⑥ Volume = _____

$h_1 = 9$ cm
$h_2 = 5$ cm
h_1
14 cm
h_2
7 cm
11 cm
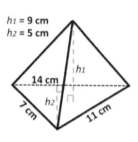

⑦ Volume = _____

3 cm
17 cm
19 cm
9 cm
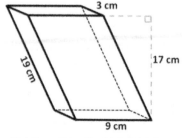

⑧ Volume = _____

25 cm
33 cm
33 cm
42 cm
7 cm
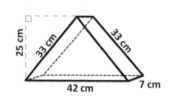

⑨ Volume = _____

10 cm
8 cm
8 cm

Name: _____

Score:

① Volume = _____

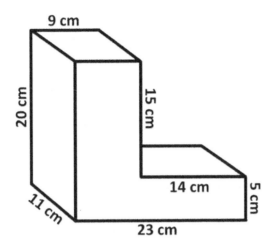

9 cm

20 cm

15 cm

14 cm

5 cm

11 cm

23 cm

_____

② Volume = _____

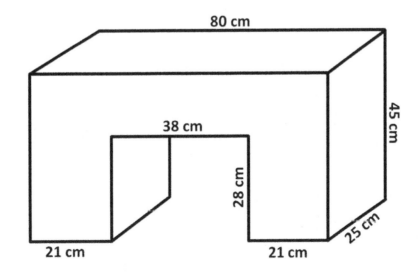

80 cm

38 cm

28 cm

45 cm

25 cm

21 cm

21 cm

Name: _____

Score:

① Volume = _____

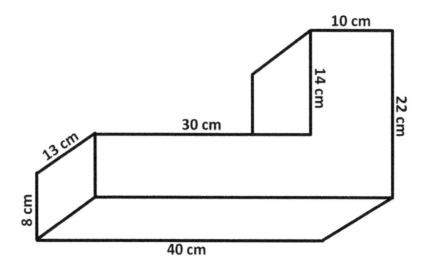

② Volume = _____

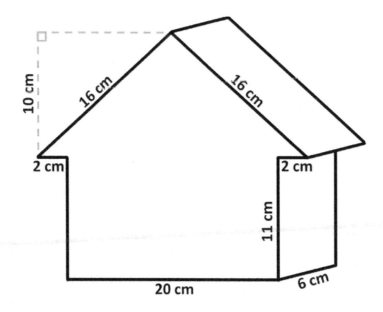

① Volume = _____

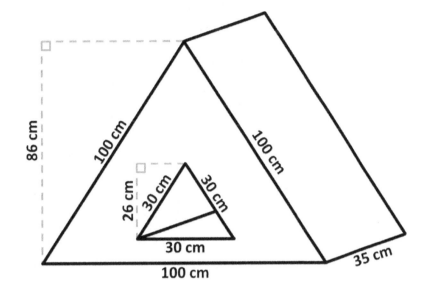

② Volume = _____

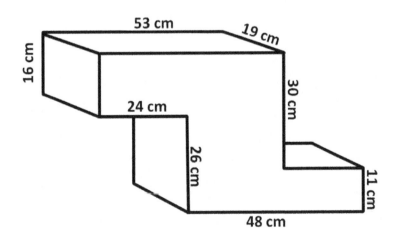

Name: _____

Score:

Have 3.14 represent π when calculating each problem. Round each answer to the nearest hundredth.

①

Volume = _____

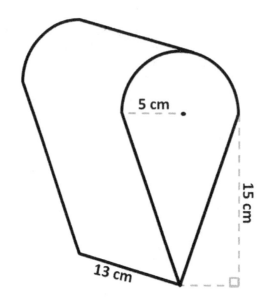

5 cm

15 cm

13 cm

②

Volume = _____

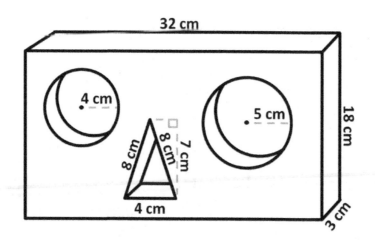

32 cm

4 cm

5 cm

8 cm

8 cm

7 cm

4 cm

18 cm

3 cm

Name: _____

Score:

Have 3.14 represent π when calculating each problem. Round each answer to the nearest hundredth.

①

Volume = _____

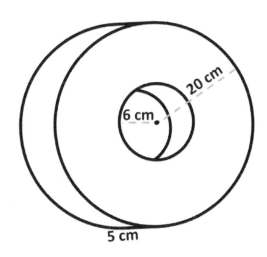

20 cm

6 cm.

5 cm

---

②

Volume = _____

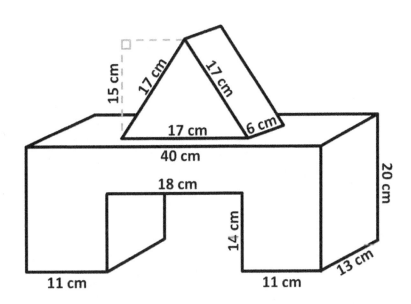

15 cm

17 cm

17 cm

17 cm

6 cm

40 cm

18 cm

14 cm

20 cm

13 cm

11 cm

11 cm

Name: _____

Score:

A **net** is 2D shape that can be folded to make 3D shape.

Match the 3D shape with its corresponding net.

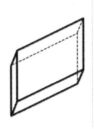

① _____

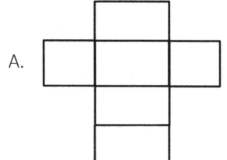

A.

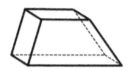

② _____

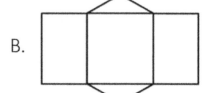

B.

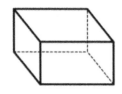

③ _____

C.

④ _____

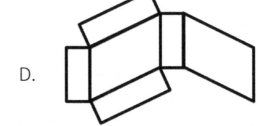

D.

⑤ _____

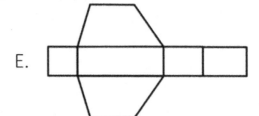

E.

Day 62
Surface Area

Name: _____

Score:

Nets can be drawn to make calculate **surface area** easier. *Calculate the area for each of the net's shapes, then add them together to find the total surface area.*

Example:

3D Shape
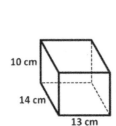

Net
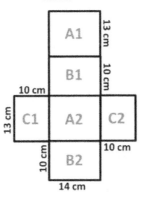

A1 = __182 cm²__

A2 = __182 cm²__

B1 = __140 cm²__

B2 = __140 cm²__

C1 = __130 cm²__

C2 = __130 cm²__

Surface Area = __904 cm²__

---

①
3D Shape

Net
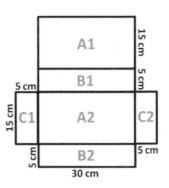

A1 = _____

A2 = _____

B1 = _____

B2 = _____

C1 = _____

C2 = _____

Surface Area = _____

---

②
3D Shape
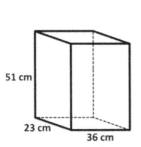

Net
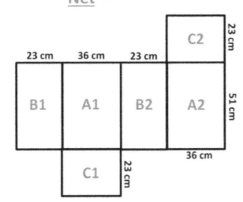

A1 = _____

A2 = _____

B1 = _____

B2 = _____

C1 = _____

C2 = _____

Surface Area = _____

© Libro Studio LLC 2020

Day 63

Surface Area

Name: _____

Score:

Refer to the measurements of the 3D shape to determine area for each of the net's shapes, then add the areas together to find the total surface area.

①

3D Shape
Net

17 cm
10 cm
7 cm

A1

B1 | C1 | B2 | C2

A2

A1 = _____
A2 = _____
B1 = _____
B2 = _____
C1 = _____
C2 = _____
Surface Area = _____

②

3D Shape
Net

10 cm
10 cm
10 cm

C1

A1 | B1 | A2 | B2

C2

A1 = _____
A2 = _____
B1 = _____
B2 = _____
C1 = _____
C2 = _____
Surface Area = _____

③

3D Shape
Net

20 cm
5 cm
5 cm

A1

B1 | C1 | B2 | A2

C2

A1 = _____
A2 = _____
B1 = _____
B2 = _____
C1 = _____
C2 = _____
Surface Area = _____

© Libro Studio LLC 2020

Day 64

Surface Area

Score:

Name: _____

*Draw your own net for each 3D shape, then calculate the surface area. (**Hint**: There are multiple ways to arrange the shapes for a net. Just make sure all the faces of the 3D shape are represented.)*

①
3D Shape   Net

17 cm, 9 cm, 8 cm

A1 = _____
A2 = _____
B1 = _____
B2 = _____
C1 = _____
C2 = _____
Surface Area = _____

②
3D Shape   Net

4 cm, 8 cm, 6 cm

A1 = _____
A2 = _____
B1 = _____
B2 = _____
C1 = _____
C2 = _____
Surface Area = _____

③
3D Shape   Net

5 cm, 13 cm, 2 cm

A1 = _____
A2 = _____
B1 = _____
B2 = _____
C1 = _____
C2 = _____
Surface Area = _____

© Libro Studio LLC 2020

Day 65
Surface Area

Name: _____

Score:

Calculate the area for each of the net's shapes, then add them to find the total surface area.

Example:

3D Shape   ### Net

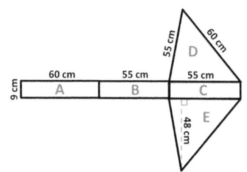

A = __540 cm²__

B = __495 cm²__

C = __495 cm²__

D = __1320 cm²__

E = __1320 cm²__

Surface Area = __4170 cm²__

---

①

3D Shape   ### Net

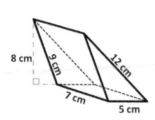

A = _____

B = _____

C = _____

D = _____

E = _____

Surface Area = _____

---

②

3D Shape   ### Net

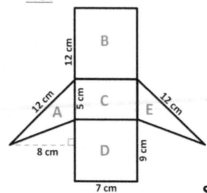

A = _____

B = _____

C = _____

D = _____

E = _____

Surface Area = _____

© Libro Studio LLC 2020

Day 66
Surface Area

Name: _____

Score:

Refer to the measurements of the 3D shape to determine area for each of the net's shapes, then add the areas together to find the total surface area.

①

3D Shape

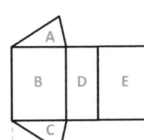

5 cm   8 cm   8 cm   13 cm   4 cm

Net

A B D E C

A = _____
B = _____
C = _____
D = _____
E = _____
Surface Area = _____

②

3D Shape

8 cm   10 cm   10 cm   10 cm   15 cm

Net

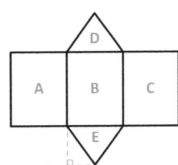

D A B C E

A = _____
B = _____
C = _____
D = _____
E = _____
Surface Area = _____

③

3D Shape

30 cm   35 cm   50 cm   50 cm   10 cm

Net

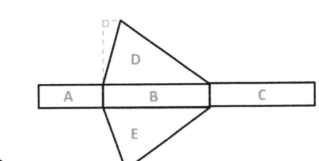

A D B C E

A = _____
B = _____
C = _____
D = _____
E = _____
Surface Area = _____

Name: _____

Score:

Draw your own net for each 3D shape, then calculate the surface area. (**Hint**: There are multiple ways to arrange the shapes for a net. Just make sure all the faces of the 3D shape are represented.)

①

3D Shape   **Net**

A = _____

B = _____

C = _____

D = _____

E = _____

Surface Area = _____

6 cm, 9 cm, 9 cm, 11 cm, 16 cm

②

3D Shape   **Net**

A = _____

B = _____

C = _____

D = _____

E = _____

Surface Area = _____

5 cm, 6 cm, 9 cm, 5 cm, 5 cm

③

3D Shape   **Net**

A = _____

B = _____

C = _____

D = _____

E = _____

Surface Area = _____

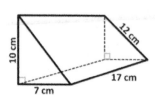

10 cm, 12 cm, 17 cm, 7 cm

Day 68
Surface Area

Name: _____

Score:

Calculate the area for each of the net's shapes, then add them to find the total surface area.

Example:

3D Shape

Net

24 cm
C1
30 cm
24 cm   30 cm   24 cm   30 cm
| A1 | B1 | A2 | B2 |
12 cm
30 cm   C2   15 cm
24 cm

30 cm
15 cm
12 cm
24 cm

$A1 = \underline{288\ cm^2}$

$A2 = \underline{288\ cm^2}$

$B1 = \underline{360\ cm^2}$

$B2 = \underline{360\ cm^2}$

$C1 = \underline{360\ cm^2}$

$C2 = \underline{360\ cm^2}$

Surface Area $= \underline{2016\ cm^2}$

---

①

3D Shape

Net

C1
12 cm
B2
32 cm
A2
12 cm
25 cm
A1   B1   C2
16 cm   12 cm   16 cm

25 cm
32 cm
12 cm
16 cm

$A1 = \underline{\hspace{2cm}}$

$A2 = \underline{\hspace{2cm}}$

$B1 = \underline{\hspace{2cm}}$

$B2 = \underline{\hspace{2cm}}$

$C1 = \underline{\hspace{2cm}}$

$C2 = \underline{\hspace{2cm}}$

Surface Area $= \underline{\hspace{2cm}}$

---

②

3D Shape

Net

27 cm
16 cm
16 cm
C1
7 cm
| A1 | B1 | A2 | B2 |
16 cm   27 cm
27 cm
10 cm   C2
16 cm

7 cm
16 cm
10 cm
27 cm

$A1 = \underline{\hspace{2cm}}$

$A2 = \underline{\hspace{2cm}}$

$B1 = \underline{\hspace{2cm}}$

$B2 = \underline{\hspace{2cm}}$

$C1 = \underline{\hspace{2cm}}$

$C2 = \underline{\hspace{2cm}}$

Surface Area $= \underline{\hspace{2cm}}$

Name: _____

Score:

Refer to the measurements of the 3D shape to determine area for each of the net's shapes, then add the areas together to find the total surface area.

①

3D Shape   **Net**

7 cm   3 cm

9 cm   10 cm

A1 = _____

A2 = _____

B1 = _____

B2 = _____

C1 = _____

C2 = _____

Surface Area = _____

②

3D Shape   **Net**

3 cm

13 cm   16 cm

16 cm

A1 = _____

A2 = _____

B1 = _____

B2 = _____

C1 = _____

C2 = _____

Surface Area = _____

③

3D Shape   **Net**

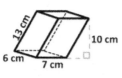

13 cm   10 cm

6 cm   7 cm

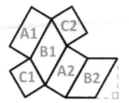

A1 = _____

A2 = _____

B1 = _____

B2 = _____

C1 = _____

C2 = _____

Surface Area = _____

Name: _____

Score:

Draw your own net for each 3D shape, then calculate the surface area. (**Hint**: There are multiple ways to arrange the shapes for a net. Just make sure all the faces of the 3D shape are represented.)

①

3D Shape   Net

12 cm
6 cm
9 cm   5 cm

A1 = _____

A2 = _____

B1 = _____

B2 = _____

C1 = _____

C2 = _____

Surface Area = _____

②

3D Shape   Net

27 cm
25 cm
2 cm   25 cm

A1 = _____

A2 = _____

B1 = _____

B2 = _____

C1 = _____

C2 = _____

Surface Area = _____

③

3D Shape   Net

32 cm
28 cm
14 cm   17 cm

A1 = _____

A2 = _____

B1 = _____

B2 = _____

C1 = _____

C2 = _____

Surface Area = _____

Calculate the area for each of the net's shapes, then add them to find the total surface area.

Example:

3D Shape	Net	
		A1 = __140 cm²__
		A2 = __140 cm²__
		B = __75 cm²__
		C = __50 cm²__
		D = __125 cm²__
		E = __40 cm²__
		Surface Area = __570 cm²__

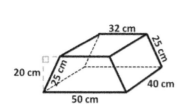

---

①

3D Shape   Net

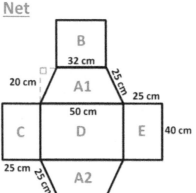

A1 = _____

A2 = _____

B = _____

C = _____

D = _____

E = _____

Surface Area = _____

---

②

3D Shape   Net

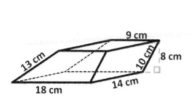
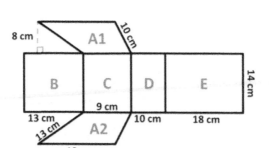

A1 = _____

A2 = _____

B = _____

C = _____

D = _____

E = _____

Surface Area = _____

© Libro Studio LLC 2020

Name: _____

Score:

Refer to the measurements of the 3D shape to determine area for each of the net's shapes, then add the areas together to find the total surface area.

①

3D Shape

Net

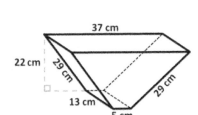

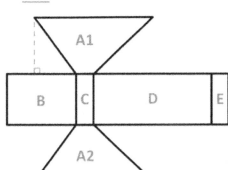

A1 = _____

A2 = _____

B = _____

C = _____

D = _____

E = _____

Surface Area = _____

②

3D Shape

Net

A1 = _____

A2 = _____

B = _____

C = _____

D = _____

E = _____

Surface Area = _____

③

3D Shape

Net

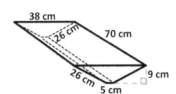

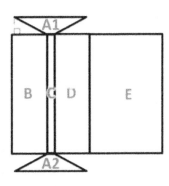

A1 = _____

A2 = _____

B = _____

C = _____

D = _____

E = _____

Surface Area = _____

© Libro Studio LLC 2020

Name: _____

Score:

*Draw your own net for each 3D shape, then calculate the surface area. (**Hint**: There are multiple ways to arrange the shapes for a net. Just make sure all the faces of the 3D shape are represented.)*

①

3D Shape   **Net**

51 cm
6 cm
35 cm
33 cm
38 cm
45 cm

A1 = _____

A2 = _____

B = _____

C = _____

D = _____

E = _____

Surface Area = _____

---

②

3D Shape   **Net**

18 cm
4 cm
18 cm
14 cm
4 cm
3 cm

A1 = _____

A2 = _____

B = _____

C = _____

D = _____

E = _____

Surface Area = _____

---

③

3D Shape   **Net**

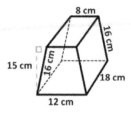

8 cm
16 cm
15 cm
16 cm
18 cm
12 cm

A1 = _____

A2 = _____

B = _____

C = _____

D = _____

E = _____

Surface Area = _____

Name: _____

A cylinder's net consists of two circles and a rectangle.
(The length of the rectangle is the circumference of the circle).
Calculate the area for each of the net's shapes, then add them to find the total surface area.
Have 3.14 represent π when calculating each problem. Round each answer to the nearest hundredth.

Example:

3D Shape	Net

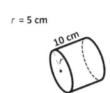

$r = 5$ cm
10 cm

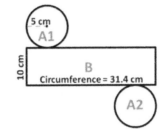

5 cm
A1
10 cm
B
Circumference = 31.4 cm
A2

A1 = __78.5 cm²__

A2 = __78.5 cm²__

B = __314.2 cm²__

Surface Area = __471.2 cm²__

---

①

3D Shape	Net

$d = 40$ cm
20 cm

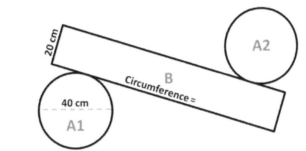

20 cm
40 cm
A1
B
Circumference =
A2

A1 = _____

A2 = _____

B = _____

Surface Area = _____

---

②

3D Shape	Net

$r = 15$ cm
8 cm

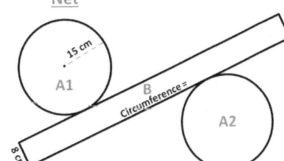

15 cm
A1
8 cm
B
Circumference =
A2

A1 = _____

A2 = _____

B = _____

Surface Area = _____

Refer to the measurements of the 3D shape to determine area for each of the net's shapes,
then add the areas together to find the total surface area.
Have 3.14 represent π when calculating each problem. Round each answer to the nearest hundredth.

①

3D Shape   **Net**

$d = 12$ cm
16 cm

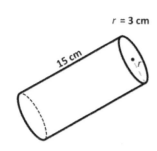

A1
B
A2

A1 = _____

A2 = _____

B = _____

Surface Area = _____

---

②

3D Shape   **Net**

$r = 3$ cm
15 cm

3 cm
A2
B
A1

A1 = _____

A2 = _____

B = _____

Surface Area = _____

---

③

3D Shape   **Net**

$r = 3$ cm
1 cm

A2
B
A1

A1 = _____

A2 = _____

B = _____

Surface Area = _____

© Libro Studio LLC 2020

Name: _____

Refer to the measurements of the 3D shape to determine area for each of the net's shapes, then add the areas together to find the total surface area.
Have 3.14 represent π when calculating each problem. Round each answer to the nearest hundredth.

①

<u>3D Shape</u>   <u>Net</u>

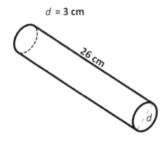

d = 3 cm

26 cm

d

A1 = _____

A2 = _____

B = _____

Surface Area = _____

②

<u>3D Shape</u>   <u>Net</u>

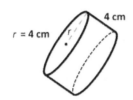

4 cm

r = 4 cm

A1 = _____

A2 = _____

B = _____

Surface Area = _____

③

<u>3D Shape</u>   <u>Net</u>

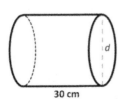

d = 24 cm

d

30 cm

A1 = _____

A2 = _____

B = _____

Surface Area = _____

Name: _____

Score:

Spheres

Surface Area

4 times pi times radius squared.

Surface Area $= 4 \times \pi \times r^2$

$SA = 4\pi r^2$

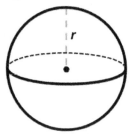

(π is about 3.14)

Have 3.14 represent π when calculating each problem. Round each answer to the nearest hundredth.

① Surface Area = _____

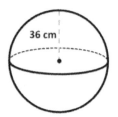

36 cm

② Surface Area = _____

1 cm

③ Surface Area = _____

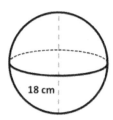

18 cm

④ Surface Area = _____

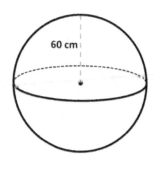

60 cm

⑤ Surface Area = _____

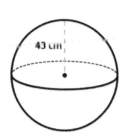

43 cm

⑥ Surface Area = _____

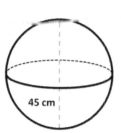

45 cm

Day 78

Surface Area

Name: _____

Score:

Have 3.14 represent π when calculating each problem. Round each answer to the nearest hundredth.

① Surface Area = _____

2 cm

② Surface Area = _____

6 cm

③ Surface Area = _____

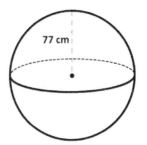

77 cm

④ Surface Area = _____

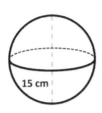

15 cm

⑤ Surface Area = _____

7 cm

⑥ Surface Area = _____

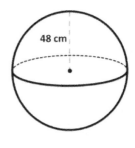

48 cm

⑦ Surface Area = _____

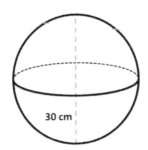

30 cm

⑧ Surface Area = _____

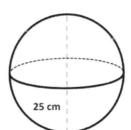

25 cm

⑨ Surface Area = _____

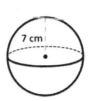

7 cm

Name: _____

Score:

Have 3.14 represent π when calculating each problem. Round each answer to the nearest hundredth.

① Surface Area = _____

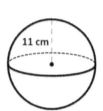

11 cm

② Surface Area = _____

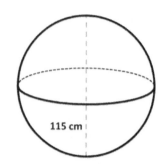

115 cm

③ Surface Area = _____

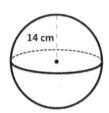

14 cm

④ Surface Area = _____

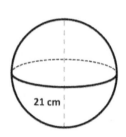

21 cm

⑤ Surface Area = _____

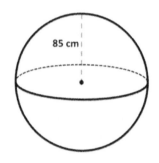

85 cm

⑥ Surface Area = _____

4 cm

⑦ Surface Area = _____

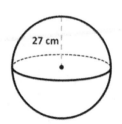

27 cm

⑧ Surface Area = _____

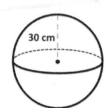

30 cm

⑨ Surface Area = _____

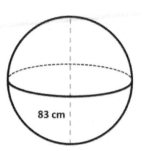

83 cm

Name: _____

Score:

Draw your own net for each 3D shape, then calculate the surface area. (**Hint**: There are multiple ways to arrange the shapes for a net. Just make sure all the faces of the 3D shape are represented.)

①
3D Shape   **Net**

8 cm   13 cm   17 cm

A1 = _____

A2 = _____

B = _____

C = _____

D = _____

E = _____

Surface Area = _____

---

②
3D Shape   **Net**

25 cm   33 cm   33 cm   42 cm   7 cm

A1 = _____

A2 = _____

B = _____

C = _____

D = _____

Surface Area = _____

---

③
3D Shape   **Net**

10 cm   48 cm   42 cm   48 cm   53 cm   36 cm

A1 = _____

A2 = _____

B = _____

C = _____

D = _____

E = _____

Surface Area = _____

Name: _____

Score:

Draw your own net for each 3D shape, then calculate the surface area. (**Hint**: There are multiple ways to arrange the shapes for a net. Just make sure all the faces of the 3D shape are represented.)

①

3D Shape   **Net**

1 cm
6 cm
5 cm
3 cm

A1 = _____

A2 = _____

B = _____

C = _____

D = _____

E = _____

Surface Area = _____

---

②

3D Shape   **Net**

20 cm
27 cm
26 cm

A1 = _____

A2 = _____

B = _____

C = _____

D = _____

E = _____

Surface Area = _____

---

③

3D Shape   **Net**

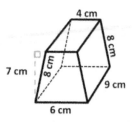

4 cm
8 cm
7 cm
8 cm
9 cm
6 cm

A1 = _____

A2 = _____

B = _____

C = _____

D = _____

E = _____

Surface Area = _____

Name: _____

Score:

Draw your own net for each 3D shape, then calculate the surface area. **(Hint**: There are multiple ways to arrange the shapes for a net. Just make sure all the faces of the 3D shape are represented.*)*

①
3D Shape   **Net**

A1 = _____

A2 = _____

B = _____

C = _____

D = _____

Surface Area = _____

(triangular prism: 19 cm, 19 cm, 14 cm, 23 cm, 16 cm)

---

②
3D Shape   **Net**

d = **32 cm**

16 cm

A1 = _____

A2 = _____

B = _____

Surface Area = _____

---

③
3D Shape   **Net**

A1 = _____

A2 = _____

B = _____

C = _____

D = _____

E = _____

Surface Area = _____

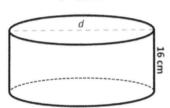

(prism: 10 cm, 5 cm, 8 cm, 4 cm)

Name: _____

Score:

*Draw your own net for each 3D shape, then calculate the surface area. (**Hint**: There are multiple ways to arrange the shapes for a net. Just make sure all the faces of the 3D shape are represented.)*

①

3D Shape   **Net**

3 cm
1 cm
8 cm

A1 = _____
A2 = _____
B = _____
C = _____
D = _____
E = _____
Surface Area = _____

②

3D Shape   **Net**

16 cm
20 cm   20 cm
24 cm   36 cm

A1 = _____
A2 = _____
B = _____
C = _____
D = _____
Surface Area = _____

③

3D Shape   **Net**

r = 10 cm

25 cm

A1 = _____
A2 = _____
B = _____
Surface Area = _____

© Libro Studio LLC 2020

Name: _____

Score:

*Draw your own net for each 3D shape, then calculate the surface area. (**Hint**: There are multiple ways to arrange the shapes for a net. Just make sure all the faces of the 3D shape are represented.)*

①

3D Shape   Net

15 cm / 12 cm / 10 cm / 12 cm / 17 cm / 22 cm

A1 = _____
A2 = _____
B = _____
C = _____
D = _____
E = _____
Surface Area = _____

②

3D Shape   Net

15 cm / 13 cm / 7 cm / 8 cm

A1 = _____
A2 = _____
B = _____
C = _____
D = _____
E = _____
Surface Area = _____

③

3D Shape   Net

5 cm / 12 cm / 6 cm / 12 cm / 20 cm

A1 = _____
A2 = _____
B = _____
C = _____
D = _____
Surface Area = _____

Name: _____

Score:

*Draw your own net for each 3D shape, then calculate the surface area. (**Hint**: There are multiple ways to arrange the shapes for a net. Just make sure all the faces of the 3D shape are represented.)*

①

3D Shape   **Net**

$A1 =$ _____

$A2 =$ _____

$B =$ _____

$C =$ _____

$D =$ _____

$E =$ _____

Surface Area = _____

10 cm
12 cm
15 cm

②

3D Shape   **Net**

$d = 6$ cm

50 cm
d

$A1 =$ _____

$A2 =$ _____

$B =$ _____

Surface Area = _____

③

3D Shape   **Net**

$A1 =$ _____

$A2 =$ _____

$B =$ _____

$C =$ _____

$D =$ _____

$E =$ _____

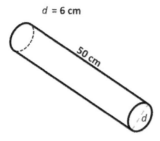

4 cm
5 cm
7 cm
15 cm

Surface Area = _____

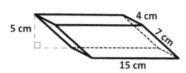

Name: _____

Score:

Draw your own net for each 3D shape, then calculate the surface area. (**Hint**: There are multiple ways to arrange the shapes for a net. Just make sure all the faces of the 3D shape are represented.)

① **3D Shape**   **Net**

9 cm   10 cm   10 cm   7 cm   13 cm

A1 = _____

A2 = _____

B = _____

C = _____

D = _____

Surface Area = _____

② **3D Shape**   **Net**

30 cm   10 cm   70 cm

A1 = _____

A2 = _____

B = _____

C = _____

D = _____

E = _____

Surface Area = _____

③ **3D Shape**   **Net**

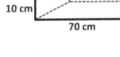

10 cm   28 cm   18 cm   18 cm   24 cm

A1 = _____

A2 = _____

B = _____

C = _____

D = _____

E = _____

Surface Area = _____

Name: _____

Score:

Draw your own net for each 3D shape, then calculate the surface area. **(Hint**: There are multiple ways to arrange the shapes for a net. Just make sure all the faces of the 3D shape are represented.*)*

①

3D Shape   **Net**

12 cm
23 cm
18 cm   10 cm

A1 = _____

A2 = _____

B = _____

C = _____

D = _____

E = _____

Surface Area = _____

---

②

3D Shape   **Net**

10 cm
8 cm
8 cm

A1 = _____

A2 = _____

B = _____

C = _____

D = _____

E = _____

Surface Area = _____

---

③

3D Shape   **Net**

3 cm
5 cm
5 cm
8 cm   11 cm

A1 = _____

A2 = _____

B = _____

C = _____

D = _____

Surface Area = _____

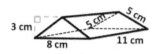

Name: _____

Score:

Draw your own net for each 3D shape, then calculate the surface area. (**Hint**: There are multiple ways to arrange the shapes for a net. Just make sure all the faces of the 3D shape are represented.)

① **3D Shape**   **Net**

4 cm   5 cm   5 cm   5 cm   7 cm

A1 = _____

A2 = _____

B = _____

C = _____

D = _____

Surface Area = _____

② **3D Shape**   **Net**

r = 12 cm

7 cm

A1 = _____

A2 = _____

B = _____

Surface Area = _____

③ **3D Shape**   **Net**

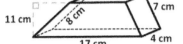

8 cm   7 cm   11 cm   8 cm   17 cm   4 cm

A1 = _____

A2 = _____

B = _____

C = _____

D = _____

E = _____

Surface Area = _____

Name: _____

Score:

Draw your own net for each 3D shape, then calculate the surface area. (**Hint**: There are multiple ways to arrange the shapes for a net. Just make sure all the faces of the 3D shape are represented.)

①

3D Shape   Net

20 cm
16 cm
9 cm
11 cm

A1 = _____

A2 = _____

B = _____

C = _____

D = _____

E = _____

Surface Area = _____

②

3D Shape   Net

30 cm
13 cm
17 cm

A1 = _____

A2 = _____

B = _____

C = _____

D = _____

E = _____

Surface Area = _____

③

3D Shape   Net

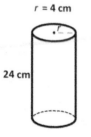

r = 4 cm

24 cm

A1 = _____

A2 = _____

B = _____

Surface Area = _____

Name: _____

Score:

① Surface Area = _____

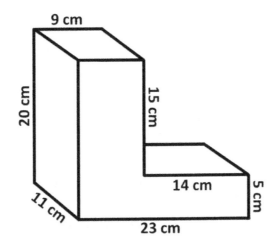

② Surface Area = _____

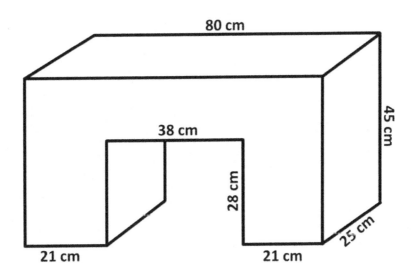

①

Surface Area = _____

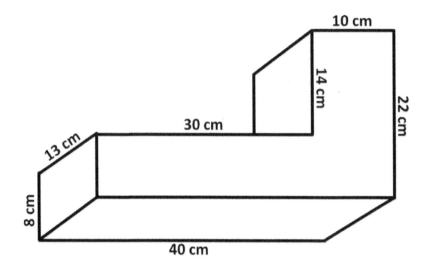

②

Surface Area = _____

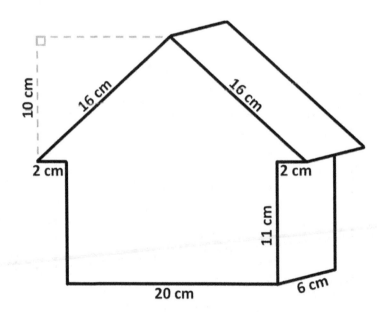

Name: _____

Have 3.14 represent π when calculating each problem. Round each answer to the nearest hundredth.

①

Surface Area = _____

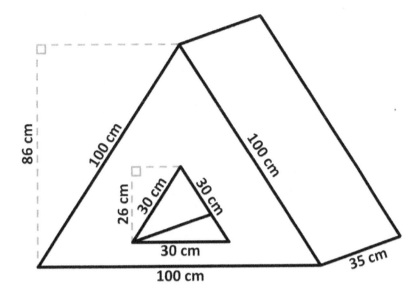

②

Surface Area = _____

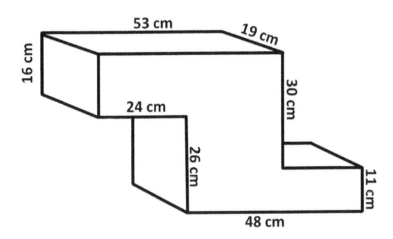

Name: _____

Score:

Have 3.14 represent π when calculating each problem. Round each answer to the nearest hundredth.

①
Surface Area = _____

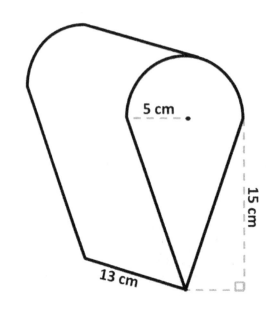

5 cm

15 cm

13 cm

②
Surface Area = _____

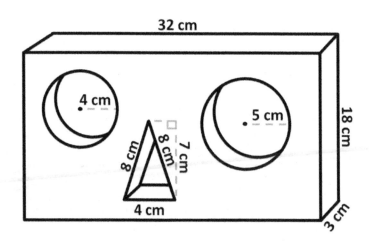

32 cm

4 cm

5 cm

8 cm

8 cm

7 cm

4 cm

18 cm

3 cm

Name: _____

Score:

Have 3.14 represent π when calculating each problem. Round each answer to the nearest hundredth.

① Surface Area = _____

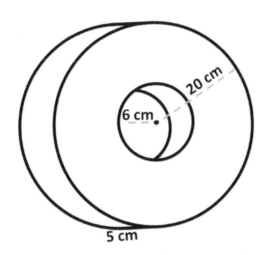

② Surface Area = _____

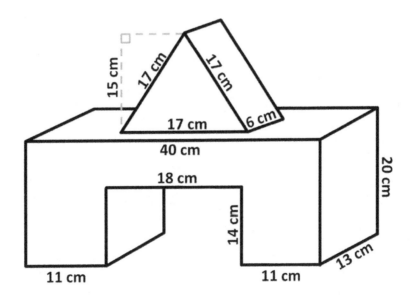

Name: _____

① Beth has a rectangular fish aquarium that is 45 cm long, 30 cm wide, and 30 cm tall. What is the surface area of the four glass sides of the aquarium?

② The water in the aquarium is 18 cm deep. What is the volume of the water? *(Refer to the information in question 1)*

③ How many more cubic centimeters of water could be added without the aquarium overflowing?
(Refer to the information in questions 1 and 2)

④ Beth is thinking about buying a larger fish aquarium. This aquarium is 75 cm by 30cm by 40 cm. How much water could this aquarium hold?

⑤ How much more water can the large fish tank hold than the one Beth currently owns?
(Refer to the information in previous questions)

Name: _____

Score:

Have 3.14 represent π when calculating each problem. Round each answer to the nearest hundredth.

① The goalie needs to stop the ball from entering the goal.
Each goal has a rectangular opening that is 8 feet by 24 feet.
What is the area of the opening?

② The playing field is 125 meters long and 85 meters wide. What is the perimeter of the field?

③ A football (soccer ball) has a diameter of about 22 cm.
What is the volume of the ball?

④ Kickoffs take place from the center circle. This circle has a 10-yard radius. What is the area of the center circle?

⑤ What is the circumference of the center circle?
(Refer to the information in question 4)

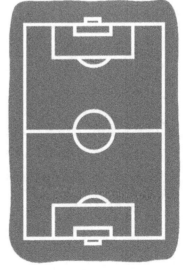

Name: _____

Score:

① A new playground is being built. The play space will be a square with 20-meter sides. What is the perimeter of this space?

② A fence will be built on three sides of the play space to keep little kids from wondering away. If each section of fence is 2 meters long, how many sections will the builders need?

③ What is the area of the play space?
(Refer to the information in question 1)

④ Dump trucks are carrying sand to the new playground.
Each truck has a rectangular box that is 5 meters by 2 meters by 3 meters. How many cubic meters of sand can each truck hold?

⑤ Each dump truck holds enough sand to cover an area of 50 square meters of the playground. How many dump truck loads of sand will it take to cover the entire play area?
(Refer to your answer for question 3)

Name: _____

Score:

Have 3.14 represent π when calculating each problem. Round each answer to the nearest hundredth.

① Jason has a garden that is 2 meters by 7 meters. He wants to build a fence around it but only has 16 meters of fencing. How much more fencing does he need to enclose the garden?

② Instead of buying more fencing, Jason decides to change the shape of his garden. He makes the garden 4 meters by 4 meters. What is the area of this new garden?

③ How much more area does the new garden have than his old garden?
(Refer to the information in questions 1 and 2)

④ Jason has a cylinder-shaped bucket that he uses to water his garden. It is 50 cm high and 40 cm in diameter. How much water can this bucket hold?

⑤ What is the circumference of Jason's bucket?
(Refer to the information in question 4)

Name: _____

Have 3.14 represent π when calculating each problem. Round each answer to the nearest hundredth.

① Mary is remodeling her house. She buys new carpet. It comes in a role that is shaped like a cylinder. The role is 60 cm in diameter. What is the circumference?

② When Mary unrolls the carpet, it is a large rectangle that is 5 meters by 8 meters. What is the area of the carpet?

③ Mary only needs the carpet for a room that is 4 meters by 5 meters. How much carpet will she have left over after recompeting this room? *(Refer to the information in question 2)*

④ Mary wants to paint two of the walls in the room. They are each 4 meters by 3 meters. How much area is this?

⑤ Mary only has half a can of paint. A full can of paint can cover 20 m² of surface area. Is this enough to paint the two walls?
(Refer to the information in question 4)

Name: _____

Have 3.14 represent π when calculating each problem. Round each answer to the nearest hundredth.

① Tyler bought a pool. It is shaped like a cylinder. The pool is 3 meters in diameter and is 1 and a half meters tall. How much water can it hold before overflowing?

② Tyler decides to only fill up the pool so that the water is 1 meter deep. How much water will that require?
(Refer to the information in question 1)

③ What is the circumference of the pool?
(Refer to the information in question 1)

④ Tyler blows up a red and white beachball for the pool. The ball is 28 cm in diameter. How much volume does it take for him to blow up the ball?

⑤ The beachball is smaller than Tyler expected so he buys a larger ball. The new ball is 38 cm in diameter. How much air can fit inside of the larger beach ball?

Answers

Day 1:
1) 3,150 cm², 250 cm 2) 27 cm², 24 cm
3) 600 cm², 100 cm 4) 44 cm², 48 cm
5) 165 cm², 52 cm 6) 100 cm², 40 cm

Day 2:
1) 608 cm², 108 cm 2) 63 cm², 32 cm
3) 6 cm², 10 cm 4) 105 cm², 44 cm
5) 108 cm², 54 cm 6) 42 cm², 34 cm
7) 204 cm², 58 cm² 8) 1,353 cm², 148 cm
9) 6 cm², 14 cm

Day 3:
1) 484 cm², 88 cm 2) 1,692 cm², 166 cm
3) 752 cm², 126 cm 4) 130 cm², 62 cm
5) 49 cm², 28 cm 6) 198 cm², 58 cm
7) 2,580 cm², 206 cm 8) 16 cm², 34 cm
9) 15 cm², 16 cm

Day 4:
1) 4 cm², 8 cm 2) 27 cm², 24 cm
3) 30 cm², 22 cm 4) 10 cm², 14 cm
5) 112 cm², 44 cm 6) 256 cm², 64 cm
7) 210 cm² , 94 cm 8) 2,700 cm², 210 cm
9) 150 cm², 50 cm

Day 5:
1) 1,539 cm², 176 cm 2) 25 cm², 25 cm
3) 40 cm², 42 cm 4) 31.5 cm², 25 cm
5) 60 cm², 44 cm 6) 520 cm², 104 cm

Day 6:
1) 416 cm² , 94 cm 2) 10.5 cm², 20 cm
3) 2,093 cm², 250 cm 4) 104.5 cm², 57 cm
5) 360 cm²,95 cm 6) 329 cm², 120 cm
7) 22.5 cm², 51cm 8) 1,800 cm², 196 cm
9) 28 cm², 28 cm

Day 7:
1) 15 cm², 21 cm 2) 56 cm², 39 cm
3) 55 cm², 52 cm 4) 82.5 cm², 44 cm
5) 72 cm², 45 cm 6) 280 cm², 96 cm
7) 35 cm², 34 cm 8) 52 cm² , 39 cm
9) 45 cm², 44 cm

Day 8:
1) 198 cm², 69 cm 2) 112.5 cm², 68 cm
3) 297 cm², 81 cm 4) 96 cm² , 51 cm
5) 135 cm²,67 cm 6) 132 cm², 61 cm
7) 31.5 cm², 35 cm 8) 675 cm², 138 cm
9) 12 cm², 21 cm

Day 9:
1) 18 cm², 26 cm 2) 20 cm², 25 cm
3) 320 cm², 82 cm 4) 96 cm², 54 cm
5) 71.5 cm² , 39 cm 6) 42 cm², 46 cm
7) 805 cm², 120 cm 8) 16.5 cm, 24 cm
9) 2030 cm², 205 cm

Day 10:
1) 2,250 cm², 200 cm 2) 500 cm², 92 cm
3) 720 cm², 128 cm 4) 450 cm², 96 cm
5) 84 cm² , 56 cm 6) 301 cm², 102 cm

Day 11:
1) 1188 cm², 148 cm 2) 1248 cm², 158 cm
3) 333 cm², 96 cm 4) 972 cm², 132 cm
5) 92 cm², 60 cm 6) 480 cm², 96 cm
7) 64 cm², 44 cm 8) 1110 cm², 164 cm
9) 1,519 cm², 172 cm

Day 12:
1) 32 cm², 28 cm 2) 75 cm², 42 cm
3) 828 cm², 140 cm 4) 2,250 cm², 196 cm
5) 42 cm², 40 cm 6) 336 cm², 86 cm
7) 12 cm², 18 cm 8) 168 cm², 62 cm
9) 1,350 cm², 170 cm

Day 13:
1) 425 cm², 88 cm 2) 97.5 cm², 45 cm
3) 18 cm² , 20 cm 4) 105 cm², 60 cm
5) 220 cm², 68 cm 6) 400 cm², 84 cm

Day 14:
1) 99 cm², 47 cm 2) 105 cm², 49 cm
3) 115 cm², 44 cm 4) 646 cm², 114 cm
5) 99 cm², 44 cm 6) 80.5 cm², 53 cm
7) 84 cm², 54 cm 8) 380 cm², 94 cm
9) 245 cm², 77 cm

Day 15:
1) 186 cm², 61 cm 2) 300 cm², 77 cm
3) 52 cm², 41 cm 4) 240 cm², 68 cm
5) 33 cm², 39 cm 6) 18 cm², 24 cm
7) 129.5 cm², 60 cm 8) 66.5 cm², 41 cm
9) 81 cm², 44 cm

Day 16:
1) 1,7662.5 cm², 471 cm
2) 4,069.44 cm², 226.08 cm
3) 1,519.76 cm², 138.16 cm
4) 3,215.36 cm², 200.96 cm
5) 22,686.5 cm², 533.8 cm
6) 530.66 cm², 81.64 cm

Day 17:
1) 7,850 cm², 314 cm
2) 15,386 cm², 439.6 cm
3) 452.16 cm², 75.36 cm
4) 113.04 cm², 37.68 cm
5) 50.24 cm², 25.12 cm
6) 78.5 cm², 31.4 cm
7) 567,162.5 cm², 2,669 cm
8) 13,266.5 cm², 408.2 cm
9) 0.785 cm², 3.14 cm

Day 18:
1) 907.46 cm², 106.76 cm
2) 254.34 cm², 56.52 cm
3) 11,304 cm², 376.8 cm
4) 200.96 cm², 50.24 cm
5) 25,434 cm², 565.2 cm
6) 63.585 cm², 28.26 cm
7) 15,828.74 cm², 445.88 cm
8) 785,000 cm², 3140 cm
9) 31,400 cm², 628 cm

Day 19:
1) 4,415.625 cm², 235.5 cm
2) 1,962.5 cm², 157 cm
3) 615.44 cm², 87.92 cm
4) 3,419.46 cm², 207.24 cm
5) 706.5 cm², 94.2 cm
6) 5,671.625 cm², 266.9 cm
7) 180,864 cm², 1507.2 cm
8) 282,600 cm², 1884 cm
9) 346.185 cm², 65.94 cm

Day 20:
1) 49 cm², 28 cm 2) 12.56 cm², 12.56 cm
3) 620 cm², 148 cm 4) 1,350 cm², 177 cm
5) 1,100 cm², 150 cm 6) 160 cm², 84 cm
7) 240 cm², 62 cm 8) 262.5 cm², 73 cm
9) 3,215.36 cm², 200.96 cm

Day 21:
1) 7,850 cm², 314 cm 2) 80 cm², 36 cm
3) 120 cm², 60 cm 4) 204 cm², 62 cm
5) 176.625 cm², 47.1 cm 6) 255 cm², 85 cm
7) 540 cm², 96 cm 8) 480 cm², 88 cm
9) 1,400 cm² , 170 cm

Day 22:
1) 0.785 cm², 3.14 cm 2) 550 cm², 135 cm
3) 225 cm², 68 cm 4) 384 cm², 92 cm
5) 540 cm², 100 cm 6) 12 cm², 16 cm
7) 28.26 cm², 18.84 cm 8) 378 cm², 102 cm
9) 240 cm², 80 cm

Day 23:
1) 6 cm², 10 cm 2) 207 cm², 83 cm
3) 375 cm², 84 cm 4) 170 cm², 81 cm
5) 14,519.36 cm², 427.04 cm 6) 161 cm², 60 cm
7) 936 cm², 126 cm 8) 139.5 cm², 57 cm
9) 6,936.26 cm², 295.16 cm

Day 24:
1) 960 cm², 166 cm 2) 928 cm², 122 cm
3) 10,930.34 cm², 370.54 cm 4) 220 cm², 62 cm
5) 70,650 cm², 942 cm 6) 1925 cm², 180 cm
7) 256 cm², 64 cm 8) 25,434 cm², 565.2 cm
9) 25 cm², 25 cm

Day 25:
1) 113 cm² 2) 298 cm² 3) 363 cm²
4) 723.77 cm² 5) 1283 cm² 6) 868.06 cm²

Day 26:
1) 1,219 cm² 2) 1,280 cm² 3) 378 cm²
4) 914 cm² 5) 294 cm² 6) 780 cm²

Day 27:
1) 125 cm² 2) 334 cm² 3) 435 cm²
4) 3,215.36 cm² 5) 857 cm² 6) 299 cm²

Day 28:
1) 141 cm² 2) 205 cm² 3) 157 cm²
4) 3,942.64 cm² 5) 388.76 cm² 6) 698.5 cm²

Day 29:
1) 959 cm² 2) 204.04 cm² 3) 496 cm²
4) 904.32 cm² 5) 599.94 cm² 6) 167 cm²

Day 30:
1) 15,470 cm³ 2) 1,820 cm³ 3) 2240 cm³
4) 12960 cm³ 5) 539 cm³ 6) 24,420 cm³

Day 31:
1) 4,320 cm³ 2) 15,680 cm³ 3) 420 cm³
4) 260 cm³ 5) 12,771 cm³ 6) 528 cm³
7) 5,980 cm³ 8) 2,700 cm³ 9) 27,740 cm³

Day 32:
1) 140 cm³ 2) 5,632 cm³ 3) 12 cm³
4) 408 cm³ 5) 13,545 cm³ 6) 4,400 cm³
7) 560 cm³ 8) 3,500 cm³ 9) 595 cm³

Day 33:
1) 360 cm³ 2) 1,350 cm³ 3) 1,300 cm³
4) 42,228 cm³ 5) 2,610 cm³ 6) 130 cm³
7) 8,750 cm³ 8) 62.5 cm³ 9) 625 cm³

Day 34:
1) 4,550 cm³ 2) 5,508 cm³ 3) 7,280 cm³
4) 270 cm³ 5) 420 cm³ 6) 624 cm³
7) 7,616 cm³ 8) 26,312 cm³ 9) 1,224 cm³

Day 35:
1) 96,460.8 cm³ 2) 4,615.8 cm³ 3) 351.68 cm³
4) 1,256 cm³ 5) 11,304 cm³ 6) 12,265.625 cm³

Answers

Day 36:
1) 254.34 cm³ 2) 13,564.8 cm³ 3) 1,205.76 cm³
4) 16,249.5 cm³ 5) 1,962.5 cm³ 6) 42,390 cm³
7) 769.3 cm³ 8) 183.69 cm³ 9) 76.93 cm³

Day 37:
1) 785 cm³ 2) 2813.44 cm³ 3) 615.44 cm³
4) 3,768 cm³ 5) 200.96 cm³ 6) 1,582.56 cm³
7) 6,358.5 cm³ 8) 17,662.5 cm³ 9) 1,808.64 cm³

Day 38:
1) 335,728.8 cm³ 2) 11,775 cm³ 3) 678.24 cm³
4) 12,560 cm³ 5) 628 cm³ 6) 6,358.5 cm³

Day 39:
1) 100,480 cm³ 2) 1,436.027 cm³ 3) 11,775 cm³
4) 6,123 cm³ 5) 8,373.333 cm³ 6) 226.08 cm³
7) 49,062.5 cm³ 8) 75.36 cm³ 9) 2,786.227 cm³

Day 40:
1) 3,349.333 cm³ 2) 3166.167 cm³ 3) 41,866.667 cm³
4) 2,562.24 cm³ 5) 23,550 cm³ 6) 1004.8 cm³
7) 6,803.333 cm³ 8) 128,216.667 cm³ 9) 870.827 cm³

Day 41:
1) 18,840 cm³ 2) 24,115.2 cm³ 3) 42,390 cm³
4) 2110.08 cm³ 5) 4,186.667 cm³ 6) 14,653.333 cm³
7) 40,558.333 cm³ 8) 54,950 cm³ 9) 334.944

Day 42:
1) 1,706.667 cm³ 2) 17,952 cm³ 3) 10 cm³
4) 4,000 cm³ 5) 2000 cm³ 6) 192 cm³

Day 43:
1) 2,268 cm³ 2) 4,840 cm³ 3) 26.667 cm³
4) 1,080 cm³ 5) 2 cm³ 6) 30 cm³
7) 6,528 cm³ 8) 466.667 cm³ 9) 5,400 cm³

Day 44:
1) 262.5 cm³ 2) 1,466.667 cm³ 3) 1,035 cm³
4) 56,250 cm³ 5) 1,008 cm³ 6) 11,000 cm³
7) 810 cm³ 8) 650 cm³ 9) 10 cm³

Day 45:
1) 6,573.333 cm³ 2) 105 cm³ 3) 136 cm³
4) 136 cm³ 5) 896 cm³ 6) 106.667 cm³
7) 39,200 cm³ 8) 238 cm³ 9) 8,190 cm³

Day 46:
1) 1,584 cm³ 2) 93.333 cm³ 3) 80 cm³
4) 6.667 cm³ 5) 12 cm³ 6) 18,746.667 cm³
7) 180 cm³ 8) 5,250 cm³ 9) 1,875 cm³

Day 47:
1) 2304 cm³ 2) 3,7800 cm³ 3) 30,000 cm³
4) 1,706.667 cm³ 5) 2,773.333 cm³ 6) 583.333 cm³
7) 18,900 cm³ 8) 1,120 cm³ 9) 630 cm³

Day 48:
1) 195,333.12 cm³ 2) 22,437.917 cm³
3) 332,869.307 cm³ 4) 659,249.28 cm³
5) 267,946.667 cm 6) 33.493 cm³

Day 49:
1) 1,436.027 cm³ 2) 795,924.583 cm³ 3) 4,846.59 cm³
4) 267.947 cm³ 5) 113,040 cm³ 6) 18,807.03 cm³
7) 1,203,649.92 cm³ 8) 904.32 cm³ 9) 14.13 cm³

Day 50:
1) 3,052.08 cm³ 2) 0.523 cm³ 3) 381,510 cm³
4) 4,709,430.613 cm³ 5) 57,876.48 cm³ 6) 904,320 cm³
7) 381,510 cm³ 8) 735,245.653 cm³ 9) 47,688.75 cm³

Day 51:
1) 3,165.12 cm³ 2) 93,492 cm³ 3) 80 cm³
4) 70 cm³ 5) 33.493 cm³ 6) 1,768 cm³
7) 600 cm³ 8) 8,574.293 cm³ 9) 15 cm³

Day 52:
1) 6,912 cm³ 2) 6,630 cm³ 3) 1,766.25 cm³
4) 1,466.667 cm³ 5) 1,413 cm³ 6) 14,040 cm³
7) 26,794.667 cm³ 8) 728 cm³ 9) 1,650 cm³

Day 53
1) 2035 cm³ 2) 7850 cm³ 3) 300 cm³
4) 18 cm³ 5) 351.68 cm³ 6) 409.5 cm³
7) 315 cm³ 8) 96 cm³ 9) 463,011.84 cm³

Day 54:
1) 96 cm³ 2) 1,800 cm³ 3) 160 cm³
4) 8,177.083 cm³ 5) 2,576 cm³ 6) 5,333.813 cm³
7) 132 cm³ 8) 550 cm³ 9) 12,861 cm³

Day 55:
1) 21,000 cm³ 2) 5,572.453 cm³ 3) 36,926.4 cm³
4) 3,145 cm³ 5) 3,061.5 cm³ 6) 105 cm³
7) 459 cm³ 8) 3,675 cm³ 9) 640 cm³

Day 56:
1) 2,750 cm³ 2) 63,400 cm³

Day 57:
1) 5,980 cm³ 2) 2,040 cm³

Day 58:
1) 136,850 cm³ 2) 33,858 cm³

Day 59:
1) 1,485.509 cm³ 2) 1,516.44 cm³

Day 60:
1) 5,714.8 cm³ 2) 7,889 cm³

Day 61:
1) D 2) E 3) A 4) B 5) C

Day 62:
1) A1=450 cm²
 A2=450 cm²
B1=150 cm²
B2=150 cm²
C1=75 cm²
C2=75 cm²
Surface area=1,350 cm²

 2) A1= 1836 cm²
A2=1836 cm²
B1= 1173 cm²
B2=1173 cm²
C1=828 cm²
C2=828 cm²
Surface area=7,672 cm²

Day 63:
1) A1=70 cm²
A2= 70 cm²
B1=170 cm²
B2=170 cm²
C1=119 cm²
C2 =119 cm²
Surface area= 718 cm²

2) A1=100 cm²
A2=100 cm²
B1=100 cm²
B2=100 cm²
C1=100 cm²
C2=100 cm²
Surface area=600 cm²

3) A1=100 cm²
A2=100 cm²
B1=25 cm²
B2=25 cm²
C1=100 cm²
C2=100 cm²
Surface area=450 cm²

Day 64:
1) 772 cm² 2) 208 cm² 3) 202 cm²

Day 65:
1) A=98 cm²
B=22.5 cm²
C=126 cm²
D=22.5 cm²
E=98 cm²
Surface Area = 367cm²

2) A= 20cm²
B=84cm²
C=35cm²
D=63 cm²
E=20cm²
Surface Area= 222 cm²

Day 66:
1) A=20 cm²
B=104cm²
C=20 cm²
D=52 cm²
E=104cm²
Surface area=300cm²

2) A=150cm²
B=150cm²
C=150cm²
D=40cm²
E=40cm²
Surface area=530cm²

3) A=350 cm²
B=500 cm²
C=500 cm²
D= 750 cm²
E=750 cm²
Surface Area=2,850 cm²

Day 67:
1) Surface Area=530 cm²
2) Surface Area=125 cm²
3) Surface Area=359 cm²

Day 68:
1) A1=512 cm²
A2=512 cm²
B1=300 cm²
B2=300 cm²
C1=192 cm²
C2=192 cm²
Surface Area=2,008 cm²

2) A1=112 cm²
A2=112 cm²
B1=189 cm²
B2=189 cm²
C1= 270 cm²
C2=270 cm²
Surface Area=1,142cm²

Day 69:
1) A1=21 cm²
A2=21 cm²
B1=63 cm²
B2=63 cm²
C1=30 cm²
C2=30 cm²
Surface Area=228 cm²

Answers

2) A1=48 cm²
A2=48 cm²
B1=48 cm²
B2=48 cm²
C1=208 cm²
C2=208 cm²
Surface Area=608 cm²

3) A1=60 cm²
A2=60 cm²
B1=70 cm²
B2=70 cm²
C1=42 cm²
C2=42 cm²
Surface Area=344 cm²

Day 70:
1) Surface Area=366 cm²
2) Surface Area=1,550 cm²
3) Surface Area=2,348 cm²

Day 71:
1) A1=820 cm²
A2=820 cm²
B=1,280 cm²
C=1,000 cm²
D=2,000 cm²
E=1,000 cm²
Surface Area=6920 cm²

2) A1=108 cm²
A2=108 cm²
B=182 cm²
C=126 cm²
D=140 cm²
E=252 cm²
Surface Area=916 cm²

Day 72:
1) A1=462 cm²
A2=462 cm²
B=377 cm²
C=65 cm²
D=377 cm²
E=481 cm²
Surface Area=2,224 cm²

2) A1=364 cm²
A2=364 cm²
B=280 cm²
C=680 cm²
D=440 cm²
E=360 cm²
Surface Area=2,488 cm²

3) A1=193.5 cm²
A2=193.5 cm²
B=1820 cm²
C=350 cm²
D=1,820 cm²
E=2,660 cm²
Surface Area=7,037 cm²

Day 73:
1) Surface Area=4,632 cm²
2) Surface Area=686 cm²
3) Surface Area=1,236 cm²

Day 74:
1) A1=1256 cm²
A2=1256 cm²
B=2512 cm²
Surface Area=5024 cm²

2) A1=706.5 cm²
A2=706.5 cm²
B=753.6 cm²
Surface Area=2,166.6 cm²

Day 75:
1) A1=113.04 cm²
A2=113.04 cm²
B=602.88 cm²
Surface Area=828.96 cm²

2) A1= 28.26 cm²
A2= 28.26 cm²
B= 282.6 cm²
Surface Area=339.12 cm²

3) A1= 28.26 cm²
A2= 28.26 cm²
B= 18.84 cm²
Surface Area=75.36 cm²

Day 76:
1) Surface Area=259.05 cm²
2) Surface Area=200.96 cm²
3) Surface Area=3,165.12 cm²

Day 77:
1) 16,277.76 cm² 2) 3.14 cm² 3) 1,017.36 cm²
4) 45,216 cm² 5) 23,223.44 cm² 6) 6,358.5 cm²

Day 78:
1) 50.24 cm² 2) 113.04 cm² 3) 74,468.24 cm²
4) 706.5 cm² 5) 153.86 cm² 6) 289,838.24 cm²
7) 2,826 cm² 8) 1,962.5 cm² 9) 615.44 cm²

Day 79:
1) 1,519.76 cm² 2) 41,526.5 cm² 3) 2,461.76 cm²
4) 1,384.74 cm² 5) 90,746 cm² 6) 200.96
7) 9,156.24 cm² 8) 11,304 cm²
9) 21,631.46 cm²

Day 80:
1) Surface Area=922 cm²
2) Surface Area=1,806 cm²
3) Surface Area=9,458 cm²

Day 81:
1) Surface Area=72 cm²
2) Surface Area=3,524 cm²
3) Surface Area=304 cm²

Day 82:
1) Surface Area=1,298 cm²
2) Surface Area=3,215.36 cm²
3) Surface Area=184 cm²

Day 83:
1) Surface Area=70 cm²
2) Surface Area=2,688 cm²
3) Surface Area=2,198 cm²

Day 84:
1) Surface Area=1,407 cm²
2) Surface Area=534 cm²
3) Surface Area=660 cm²

Day 85:
1) Surface Area=900 cm²
2) Surface Area=998.52 cm²
3) Surface Area=326 cm²

Day 86:
1) Surface Area=414 cm²
2) Surface Area=6,200 cm²
3) Surface Area=2,052 cm²

Day 87:
1) Surface Area=1,428 cm²
2) Surface Area=448 cm²
3) Surface Area=222 cm²

Day 88:
1) Surface Area=125 cm²
2) Surface Area=1,431.84 cm²
3) Surface Area=435 cm²

Day 89:
1) Surface Area=926 cm²
2) Surface Area=2,242 cm²
3) Surface Area=703.36 cm²

Day 90:
1) Surface Area= 1,446 cm²
2) Surface Area= 12,722 cm²

Day 91:
1) 2532 cm² 2) 1,128 cm²

Day 92:
1) 2,1470 cm² 2) 7,935 cm²

Day 93:
1) 843.196 cm² 2) 1,396.08 cm²

Day 94:
1) 3,102.32 cm²
2) 3,377 cm²

Day 95:
1) 4500 cm²
2) 24,300 cm³
3) 16,200 cm³
4) 90,000 cm³
5) 49,500 cm³

Day 96:
1) 192 ft² 2) 420 m 3) 5,572.453 cm³
4) 314 yard² 5) 62.8 yard

Day 97:
1) 80 meters
2) 30 sections
3) 400 m²
4) 30 m³
5) 8

Day 98:
1) 2 meters
2) 16 m²
3) 2 m²
4) 68,000 cm³
5) 125.6 cm

Day 99:
1) 188.4 cm 2) 40 m² 3) 20 m² 4) 24 m² 5) No

Day 100:
1) 10.597 m³
2) 7.065 m²
3) 9.42 m
4) 11,488.21 cm³
5) 28,716.347 cm³

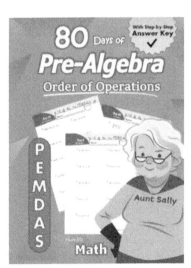

ISBN: 978-1-63578-330-8

Current contact information can be found at:
www.HumbleMath.com
www.LibroStudioLLC.com

Image credits (Day 96 football/soccer images): EKramar/Shutterstock.com

Made in the USA
Las Vegas, NV
15 June 2021